William Edgar Harding

Jake Kilrain's Life And Battles

William Edgar Harding

Jake Kilrain's Life And Battles

ISBN/EAN: 9783741134180

Manufactured in Europe, USA, Canada, Australia, Japa

Cover: Foto ©Thomas Meinert / pixelio.de

Manufactured and distributed by brebook publishing software
(www.brebook.com)

William Edgar Harding

Jake Kilrain's Life And Battles

A COMPLETE HISTORY

OF THE

GREAT INTERNATIONAL PRIZE FIGHT

WITH JEM SMITH,

for $10,000, the POLICE GAZETTE Diamond Belt and Championship of the World.

WITH ILLUSTRATIONS.

BY WILLIAM E. HARDING,

The "Police Gazette" Representative at the Great Historical Battle.

CONTENTS.

PORTRAITS.

ILLUSTRATIONS.

JAKE KILRAIN'S LIFE AND BATTLES.

SKETCH OF THE CHAMPION.

Jake Kilrain, the American champion, who fought Jem Smith for $10,000, the "Police Gazette" diamond belt and championship of the world, stands 5 feet 10½ inches high, and weighs 210 pounds. His chest measurement is 41 inches, upon and around the biceps 16 inches, forearm 14 inches, waist 34 inches, thigh 25 inches, calf of leg 16½ inches. He wears a No 9 shoe and No. 9 glove, and it takes a 17 inch collar to encircle his neck. Kilrain gives the following interesting history of his life:

"My name is Joseph John Killion. When I was a lad my comrades persisted in calling me Kilrain, and the name has stuck to me ever since, so I have bowed to the inevitable, and now write my name 'Kilrain.' I was born at Greenport, Columbia county, which is in the State of New York, and the date of my nativity is the 9th of February, 1859, so that I am twenty-eight years of age. I have no regular occupation other than training athletes and boxing, but in my younger days I worked in a rolling mill in Somerville, Mass., which is a suburb of Boston. It was here that I developed a love for athletic sports. In fact they were forced upon me, for in such a large establishment it was not to be wondered at that there were many good boxers, and as I was a gawky country boy, I was a mark for all their practical jokes. Sometimes they went too far, and when I remonstrated they laughed at me. You can bet that made me mad, so I just made up my mind that I would thrash one or two of these tormentors, and from that day I was champion of the mill.

"The first customer was Jack Daley, who had fought several small ring battles, but I put him to sleep in short order. My next encounter was with Jem Driscoll, a regular giant, who, while having little or no science, could hit with the force of a trip hammer. He hurt me very badly, but I finally wore him down, and when he at last gave up his mother would scarcely have known him. I next fought Dan Dwyer. It was a long and bloody fight, but I finally managed to pull through a winner. I was very sore for a long time and thought I was internally injured. The last man that was pitted against me was Dennis Roach. He had been imported to the mill with the idea of putting an end to young Kilrain's run of luck, and they came near doing so, too. I was not very well when the day for the fight arrived, but knowing full well that I should have been branded as a coward if I backed out, I got into the ring determined to stand up as long as I was able. My antagonist was a hurricane fighter, and sought to annihilate me in a couple of rounds. He hit me in the stomach several times, and I thought that I must give in, but after a little while Roach's blows got weaker, and finding he could not hurt me much, I fought with him, and by a judicious use of my left hand managed to close up his eyes. Roach was willing to keep on fighting, although he could not see. Finally his friends took him away, and that ended my fighting career in the mill."

He took to rowing, and was one of the winning crew in a four-oared race on Lake Waldron. This appeared to whet Kilrain's appetite for boating, and in 1883 we find him competing successfully for the Junior sculling championship at the Nati nal Amateur Regatta, held at Newark, N. J. Of course, when President Garfield, of the National Association, learned the identity of "Killion," and discovered him to be a professional pugilist, he at once took steps for an investigation, and Mr. "Killion" and

Mr. Kilrain ceased to be an amateur oarsman. His next appearance in a racing boat was on the Charles River, when he was one of a four-oared Hull boat crew. They rowed against the Middlesex and Riverside crews, and beat them both. A few weeks later on he formed part of a four-oared crew which rowed in the Union Boat Club regatta on the Charles River, and won the prize. The same crew was one of the entries in the Fourth of July regatta of 1883, but suffered defeat, rowing second to the Middlesex crew, which was accounted one of the best amateur fours.

"In the winter of 1883 I launched out as a down-right professional pugilist. I obtained a situation in the Boston Cribb Club, where I was assistant to Jem M'Carthy. Here I got more hard knocks than wealth, but I gained a good deal of experience. While employed in the Cribb Club I was called upon to face some good men. My first experience was with Harry Allen. We were to have contested six rounds, but I had Allen knocked out in the very first round. The gentlemen present asked me to 'let up' on my antagonist. This I did, and he rallied, but made such a poor showing that the management stopped the fight.

"My next antagonist was George Godfrey, the colored pugilist. This was to have been a six-round fight, but I hit the darkey so hard that he quit in the third round.

"Nothing more was done in 1883, but the following year was a busy one for me. Jim Goode was pitted against me for a six-round battle. The referee declared it a draw, but disinterested people say that I should have got the verdict, as Goode was to all intents and purposes a defeated man.

"My next antagonist was Charley Mitchell, with whom I fought a four-round draw. Then came my encounter with Mike Cleary, which was for four rounds. Despite the fact that Cleary could scarcely stand at the end of the fourth round, Billy Edwards declared the contest a draw.

"Next in order comes my meeting with Jack Burke. We were to have fought five rounds, but the first was so hot and heavy that the Boston police got on the stage and prevented us from finishing the combat; they allowed us to finish the other four rounds in a very tame sparring match. A proposition was made to Burke to settle the affair in some other city, but the Irish lad refused."

After this Kilrain took a long rest, and then he went to Bangor, Me., and met a giant by the name of Jerry Murphy, who stood six feet one inch and weighed 200 pounds. Kilrain almost killed his burly antagonist, and in the middle of the second round put him to sleep by a right-hander on the jaw.

In 1885, at Cambridge, Mass., Kilrain met William Sheriff, the Prussian. They were to have fought six rounds, but Kilrain knocked his antagonist insensible in two rounds. The latter was finally restored to consciousness, and then Kilrian sparred a light round with Sheriff who could make no showing with his man at all.

George Fryer, the English pugilist, was Kilrain's next adversary, and they fought a five-round draw. The last victim that Kilrain had in 1885 was Jem M'Glynn, of New Bedford, Mass. This individual, by the exercise of a lot of pedestrianism, managed to last through three rounds, then he got hit so hard on the jaw that he quit, refusing to go on.

During the year 1886 Kilrain had many adversaries. The first one to oppose him was Frank Herald, whom some of the New York newspapers "boosted" into such eminence. This is the pugilist of whom it was said that James Gordon Bennett offered to subscribe a purse of $2,000 to fight John L. Sullivan, provided no reporters other than his own men were allowed to see the battle. Herald and Kilrain met in Baltimore, Md., and the first-named lasted one short round, Kilrain sending in such a smashing hit on the jaw that Herald toppled over insensible.

Wm. E. Harding, the sporting editor of the POLICE GAZETTE, was referee, but because the police broke in the ring, he decided the contest a draw, but admitted that if the round had been finished and the police not stopped hostilities Kilrain would have been declared the winner, for everyone knew that Herald was whipped.

Soon after this Kilrain was hired to spar at the Theatre Comique, Philadelphia, Pa. The conditions under which he was to draw his salary were that he was to meet a fresh man every night, and either best his opponent or send him to sleep. This Kilrain did. He began on Godfrey, who got his quietus in the second round. When Godfrey was knocked down everyone thought that his neck was broken, and it was hours before he was restored to consciousness. In fact he has never been the same man since Kilrain's mighty right hand came in contact with his jaw.

Tom Kelly managed to stand up three rounds, and part of the fourth round. Then he was taken to his room in a very demoralized condition. Third on the list was Denny Killeen, who, though standing up through four rounds, was badly used up. Killeen was knocked down seven times in the quarter of an hour he faced Kilrain. This was a wonderful showing for an athlete, and the record stands unrivalled.

In 1885 Kilrain had many glove fights. His first battle was with Jack Ashton on

JAKE KILRAIN,

HERO OF THE GREAT INTERNATIONAL BATTLE, WHO ACTED AS MITCHELL'S
SECOND IN HIS CONTEST WITH SULLIVAN.

Long Island. Ashton had whipped Dick Collier and won fifteen battles, and many supposed he would easily defeat Kilrain, but Kilrain won.

"Joe Lannon, of Boston, then challenged me to fight with skin gloves. A purse was put up by the Cribb Club, Boston, and Lannon was made a big favorite, because Sullivan, who was then champion, refused to meet him. Lannon managed to stand up for 13 rounds, and then a blow on the point of the jaw made him oblivious to the call of time, and I won. Richard K. Fox, my backer, then put up $1,000 with the New York *Clipper* and offered to match me to fight John L. Sullivan for $5,000 or $10,000 a side, or any man in the world, for the 'Police Gazette' diamond belt and the championship. Sullivan could not be coaxed to fight me, and the match fell through.

"Richard K. Fox then handed me the 'Police Gazette' championship belt and matched me to fight Jem Smith, the champion of England, for $10,000 and the championship of the world."

HERE IS SMITH'S RECORD.

He was born in the parish of St. Luke's, London, England; he is 5 feet 8¼ inches high, and fights at 182 pounds; his physical measurements are as follows: Chest, 40¾ inches; waist, 36½ inches; hips, 40¼ inches; thigh, 24½ inches; calf, 16¾ inches; biceps, 15¼ inches; he has weighed, untrained, 212 pounds; he made his advent in pugilism in 1882, when he won a boxing competition open to 140-pound pugilists in London; same year he defeated Bob Preston in a bare knuckle fight in 8 rounds, occupying 20 minutes, near London, for $40; same year in London won the all-England boxing competition for 154-pound men; same year, at St. Luke's with bare knuckles, beat Liddard, middle-weight, in 6 rounds; same year beat Snavey, of Oliver, 168-pound man, with gloves, in 4 rounds; in 1883 won the open boxing competition at the Blue Anchor, Shoreditch, for middle-weights, defeating Bill Brand, Bob Preston and Arthur Cooper; same year beat Bill Davis with knuckles, near London, for $50, time of fight one hour; same year beat Henry Arnold, with gloves, for $50, near London, 14 rounds, occupying 55 minutes; same year at Barket, whipped Skidmore, a 16-stone man (224 pounds) in 3 rounds, with gloves; Dec. 17, 1884, defeated Wolff Bendoff in a hard glove fight to a finish, for $100, and won in 12 rounds. In this fight Smith broke his left arm in the third round. In 1885, in the heavy-weight glove competition, open to all comers, at the Blue Anchor, Shoreditch, beat Sugar Goodson, Wanop and Longer, the last named in the final, winning the competition; Dec. 16, 1885, at Godstone, England, for £200 a side and the ring championship of England, beat Jack Davis with bare knuckles, 4 rounds, lasting 15 minutes; Feb. 16, at Maison Lafitte, near Paris, France, for £300 and the championship of England, fought Alfred Greenfield, of Birmingham, 13 rounds. Smith had the best of the fight when Greenfield's partisans broke into the ring. Jem Mace, the referee, declared the fight a draw. Soon afterward Smith was matched to fight Jack Knifton, the 81-tonner, as he is called. The men met three times, once near Paris, France, the second time near London, and the third time in London. On the first occasion Knifton refused to fight because Smith's friends predominated, and the police broke up the fight after two meetings.

William E. Harding, sporting editor of the POLICE GAZETTE, New York, who represented Richard K. Fox, the backer of Jake Kilrain, the American champion, in his international battle with Jem Smith, the British champion, for $10,000, the "Police Gazette" diamond belt and the championship of the world, was born in Toronto, Canada, of Irish parents, June 6, 1848. He is a nephew of Ned O'Neale, the Streathem Youth, who gained fistic glory by his prowess in the prize ring.

W. E. Harding is well-known in sporting circles all over the country as an accomplished and thorough athlete, and has been made famous through his various exploits. From 1863 to 1869 he was the champion runner from one to ten miles distance, and also held the championship as a fifty-mile walker up to the month of January, 1879. He was competitor for the title, winning three trials. As a bicycle rider Mr. Harding has attained the highest place, being acknowledged as the champion for three years, respectively 1870, '71, '72. He has attended all the great fistic battles; witnessed Mike McCoole defeat Aaron Jones; was present at Tom Allen's many battles in America, and witnessed Jem Mace defeat Tom Allen, at New Orleans, in 1870, and filled the position of referee at glove contests between Charley Mitchell, Jake Kilrain and other noted exponents of the manly art. He filled the position of referee in the Paddy Smith and Jemmy Mitchell battle for the "Police Gazette" belt and light-weight championship, and arranged the prize fight between John L. Sullivan and Paddy Ryan, and represented Richard K. Fox on that occasion. Since 1867 he has been sporting editor of the New York *Daily* and *Sunday News*, whose columns are regarded as high authority on all sporting matters, and embrace all the athletic sports of the day. Since Wm. E. Harding, the once famous runner, champion walker and bicycle rider has been sporting editor of Richard K. Fox's great sporting paper, the Illustrated POLICE GAZETTE of New

York, his energy, enterprise and abilities have been well appreciated by Richard K. Fox, the "bonanza" sporting promotor of great events, from a boat race to a championship prize fight, and proprietor of the POLICE GAZETTE. On Aug. 1, 1881, Richard K. Fox presented William E. Harding with a gold watch and chain valued at $500. The "cap" bears suitable description and name of the donor. On Aug. 1, 1882, as a token of esteem from Richard K. Fox, he received a diamond collar-button, valued at $250, and a massive gold locket set with a solitaire diamond, value $100. In August, 1883, Harding received for his annual present a beautiful scarf pin, set with rubies, sapphires and diamonds, in the shape of a large "H," valued at $150: also a large gold shield, valued at $300, with the words "Police Gazette" set in diamonds and rubies beautifully inscribed. On New Year's day, 1884, he received a large solitaire diamond ring, value $800, from Richard K. Fox. On August 1, 1884, Harding received for his annual August present a large horse-shoe scarf pin, made of 22-caret gold. The seven nails are seven blue mine diamonds of great value. The toe of the shoe is set with diamonds. In the shoe calks are a large sapphire and a ruby, while from the frog of the shoe is three initial letters, "W. E. H." set with garnets and diamonds. Attached to the pin by a unique gold chain is a gold shield, which bears the following: "To William E. Harding, from Richard K. Fox, proprietor of the POLICE GAZETTE, New York, as a token of appreciation for services as sporting editor, and fidelity as a friend. August 1, 1884." In 1886 he received from Richard K. Fox an elegant gold watch, valued at $200, and on January 1, 1887, he received a pair of couplet diamond sleeve buttons, valued at $500. In every city in the United States and Canada he has received souvenirs and presents of all descriptions from sporting men with whom he is very popular. He is not proud nor arrogant, but treats everyone with respect and in a sociable manner.

GRAPHIC ACCOUNT OF JAKE KILRAIN'S WONDERFUL BATTLE WITH JEM SMITH, OF ENGLAND.

[FROM SPECIAL REPORT TO "POLICE GAZETTE."]

PARIS, Dec. 19, 1887.—Kilrain came as near whipping the champion of England to-day as a man could and still miss it. He knocked Jem Smith down thirty odd times in two hours and a half. There was no prospect of Smith winning, and every assurance that Kilrain would knock him out when the fight was called, on account of darkness ostensibly, but really because about 75 Englishmen saw the money that they had placed so radiantly on Smith going rapidly out of sight.

It was the most distinguished body of men who ever went to a mill. It cost from $200 upward to see the muscular giants pound each other into pitiable and bloody helplessness. The distinguished party left the Pelican Club in London on Sunday night and met at the Victoria Station at 8 o'clock, thence by rail to New Haven, where everybody climbed gloomily into a stuffy little boat that ran to Dieppe, in France. After the boat had made enthusiastic and earnest endeavors to turn over twice in different directions at the same time for seven long hours the distinguished party trooped ashore at Dieppe, a landing place that is famous for gloom, dampness and a breakfast of surpassing and spectacular misery. The men looked haggard and worn. It had been a wearisome crossing.

The Marquis of Queensberry wandered socially about. He is small, quietly dressed, and smooth shaven except for two patches of whiskers, and the picture of the conventional British waiter except that he is vastly more unassuming than that haughty menial. Lord De Clifford was what might be called chummy; Lord Chareton was inclined to go off into corners and stare at his boots, and Lord Mayo looked monstrously damp and solemn. Among the others were Captain Lee Barber, Col. Browne, the Hon. Michael Sandy, Arthur Cooper, Count Saville, Capt. Drummond, Mr. Mackey, Capt. Bailey, Willis Wilde, the suave six-foot brother of Oscar, and numerous others.

It was a perfectly managed affair. To be discovered meant imprisonment for the spectators as well as the principles. From point to point of the long railroad journey that followed, Mr. George Atkinson, editor of the *Sporting Life*, received messages that decided his course. Meanwhile another party, consisting of the two fighters and their seconds, journeyed west from Paris. They met at Rouen. There was another change, and the whole party journeyed on. It was now about 10 o'clock in the morning, and members of the party were so badgered and harrassed that they went this way or that as they were bid like sleepy children.

After the train had been running two hours it was discovered that four of Kilrain's

THE CHAMPION'S COLORS.

friends had been lost on the way. They were Charley Johnson, Jimmy Wakeley, Phil Lynch and W. D. Morton. They had traveled 3,000 miles to see the mill, but missed it at the last minute.

At Bonnaires the crowd streamed aboard a solitary tugboat and set off up the river Siene. There were seventy-eight Englishmen and four Americans on board. Smith was constantly surrounded by friends, but Jake Kilrain sat almost alone. His friends were Pony Moore and Charley Mitchell, and mighty good friends they proved to be later on.

The boat ran to a small and swampy island in a marshy part of the river. A twenty-four foot ring was made with stakes and ropes that had been taken along, and at 2:10 P. M. Smith ran up and bounded into the ring. He looked fit to fight for his life, and the lords and swells and millionaires cheered him to the echo.

"If you can't whip the Yankee to-day, Jimmy," yelled an enthusiastic Captain of dragoons, "you can never do it, you know."

"I'll lay 200 to 100 on Smith," yelled a lord.

"Seventy to 20 on our Jimmie," yelled another.

Everywhere the cry was for Smith. His seconds were a noisy, tricky and brutal Cockney named Jack Baldock and a man named Jack Harper. J. Fleming was time-keeper and umpire for Smith.

Kilrain walked up to the ring amid comparative silence. His face was set and determined. He knew that he was alone, but for his seconds, Charley Mitchell and Ned Donnelly, and his friend Pony Moore. Charley Rowell was Kilrain's bottle-holder. The fight was for the largest purse ever known in the prize ring. Before the battle began W. E. Harding stepped into the ring and handed Kilrain £200 to bet as he chose. It was a present from Richard K. Fox, of the POLICE GAZETTE, who backed Kilrain. The Marquis of Queensberry was to have acted as referee, and he was quite willing, too, but there was a hitch, and Mr. Atkinson took his place.

The sun came out and brightened up the scene as the men stepped out in the middle of the ring and looked each other over. They were as well matched as any pair of gladiators the world has seen. Each weighed about 180 pounds, though Kilrain was about four pounds the heavier. The men were trained fine, and their muscles played like steel fibres under satin as they moved about. Each was stripped to the waist. The waists of the men were wound in big plasters to give them strength, and resin was sprinkled over their bare and knotty hands. The water rippled round the little island, and some peasants across the river ceased ploughing their field to stare at the crowd of handsomely dressed Englishmen crowding around two half naked and magnificent-looking men. The cries for Smith rent the air. It was the most important fight since that of Heenan and Sayers, and everybody knew it.

THE FIGHT BEGINS.

The referee called time and the two combatants jumped forward. Smith swung his big arms straight in front of him and danced a bit on his pins. Kilrain, or the Yankee, as he is called, stood in an easy position with his hands well down and his shoulders back. Smith looked wicked, Kilrain confident. Smith had fought and defeated such veteran fighters as Greenfield and Davis. Kilrain had not only never been in the regular professional prize ring, but he had not even seen a bare knuckle fight. He looked as clean cut as a race horse.

Kilrain made a feint at Smith, let go a low left-hander, and then brought his left in on the Englishman's jaw with a shock like a sand-club's blow. It was an early and forcible indication that Kilrain was in earnest. Smith rushed in on him. They clinched and fell with Smith on top. The cheers of the Englishmen were deafening. Both men were picked up and carried to their corners.

FIRST BLOOD FOR KILRAIN.

2.—The men sprang at each other hotly. There was a sharp interchange of blows, and then some terrific slugging followed. Kilrain sent in a slight left-hander that split Smith's lips up and down and sent the blood spattering over his chest and arms. Harding claimed first blood for Kilrain and got it. Smith caught Kilrain a swinging right-hander that nearly ripped Kilrain's ear from his head, and sent the blood streaming over him, too. The men clinched and fell, with Smith on top.

3—Smith rushed and knocked Kilrain down, falling on him heavily. Both men were now red with blood, and Kilrain's left eye was closed.

4—When Kilrain came up for this round there was something in the expression of his good eye that caused Smith's seconds to warn him. Kilrain ducked a long blow of Smith's, and coming up, dealt the Englishman one in the neck that almost put him to sleep. He hit him again in the same place and threw him heavily by a back lock.

5 to 10—The next six rounds were precisely similar. In every one Smith received frightful punishment and was thrown at the end of each round.

SMITH'S TERRIBLE PUNISHMENT.

11—The men stood before each other in a dead silence. The Englishmen who had been backing a sure thing were startled. The hardest hitter in England was a mass of blood and bruises. Kilrain's forehead was laid open and his face swollen, but he smiled quietly as he stepped in front of his man.

"You don't think so, Jem," he said softly, "but the fight won't be yours."

Smith made a feint, and a moment later Kilrain shot out his left, and catching the Briton square on the chin knocked him flat and cold. They picked Smith up, but he seemed more dead than alive, but he rallied quickly.

It is due to Mitchell to say that but for him Kilrain would have fared very much harder. He resented every display of brutal injustice in the sharpest manner. At one point after the crowd had howled at him for backing up his principal, he jumped into the middle of the ring and shouted, shaking his fist, "You dare not maltreat my man. I blush to have to acknowledge that you are Englishmen. Here's a lade come 3,000 miles over the sea to fight your champion. He never even saw a prize fight before. He has no friends here, while there's a hundred against him. He's going to have his rights or I've got to get licked as well as he."

THE BATTERED PUGILISTS.

It would be difficult to imagine anything more revolting than the condition of the men at the end of the fight. It had grown dusky, and the spectators were shivering in the shrill winter's wind. The two magnificent athletes of three hours before were battered almost out of human semblance. Kilrain's right eye was puffed up like a miniature balloon. His left eye was battered, but still partly open, and he had a heavy cut across his nose. His jaw looked like a piece of raw beefsteak, and the bumps on his forehead stood out like eggs. A continual stream of blood flowed from his right ear where it was torn. All over his body, from the big abrasions where the resin-smeared fists of the opponent had fallen, continual sponging could not keep the blood from smearing the body. But, bad as Kilrain's appearance was, Smith's was worse. He had been pounded till his face was battered out of its former semblance, his lips had been cut by early blows of Kilrain, and each subsequent smash had puffed and swollen them violently.

AT THE RING SIDE.

LONDON, Dec. 20, 1887.

It is narrated by a spectator, a close observer, that when on the ground they manfully abstained from taking any unfair advantage and remained passive until picked up by their seconds. Occasionally, of course, there were objections and appeals to the referee by the seconds, but, although words were bandied freely about, a dash of wit turned the situation into one of the most laughable description. At one time one man waited until his opponent was rising from his seat, whereupon the following conversation took place:

Harper—Doesn't your man want to fight, Donnelly?

Donnelly—You'll not be in a hurry after a few more rounds.

Mr. Harding—Look! We claim first blood.

Harper (amid much laughter)—You've been asleep; we drew that some time ago.

Mitchell—It's a nice day, Jake. Take your time. It's ten to one on you.

Here Kilrain knocked Smith down with a terrific right-hander on the left ear, which immediately swelled up.

Donnelly—Hallo! He is getting weak.

Harper—Yes, a fortnight.

Mr. A. Cooper—Kilrain is a good man and a fair fighter too, Smith. He's a better man than ever I thought him.

After a few more rounds they clinched and wrestled for a fall, and a bystander remarked, "He can't throw him?" to which Kilrain replied, "Can't I throw him?" and over went Smith.

As they were being carried to their respective corners Mitchell said: "Look, Jake, at his ear. Don't stand their hank."

At one period the altercation between the seconds was amusing, Mitchell appealing to the referee in the 31st round:

"Here!" They are gouging my man!"

Baldock—You lie; you know I wouldn't do such a thing.

RICHARD K. FOX,

PROPRIETOR "POLICE GAZETTE," NEW YORK, BACKER OF JAKE KILRAIN AND
DONOR OF "POLICE GAZETTE" DIAMOND BELT.

Mitchell—No, John; it's a shame to accuse you of such conduct. You'll forgive me, Jack, won't you? (satirically).

Howes—Kilrain is a fighter.

Governor Fleming—He's a much better man than I thought him.

Donnelly—Let's have fair play, and may the best man win.

"Pony" Moore—You know we are in a strange country.

After the 40th round Donnelly and Baldock, who had sworn vengeance previously, went into the centre of the ring and shook hands vigorously.

Donnelly—Look, gentlemen, he walks to his corner.

Harper—That's because you can't carry him.

Baldock (to Smith, sitting in his corner)—Oh! Jem, if I had a looking glass! Anybody would kiss you. (Here Baldock suited the action to the word by kissing Smith.)

Mitchell (as Jake walked to the centre)—Keep your hands shut; come a little this way.

A Spectator—We'll want some candles soon.

Mitchell (satirically)—Look out, Jake; mind Jem's left. He changes that leg and gives an awful punch in the darby.

Harper—When he does get it there you'll not like it, take my word.

Baldock (hysterically)—Go on, Jem; your constitution can stand it.

Howes—Don't stand so much of that wrestling, Jem. (To bystander)—Kilrain's a good 'un.

Mitchell—Oh! look at poor Jem's ear. I wouldn't have that ear for all the money in the Bank of England.

Harper—Ah! wait until you meet Sullivan, Mitchell.

Donnelly—Charley, don't you think we had better give them half an hour's rest?

Harper—You'll want two before long.

Baldock—Jem, I thought we had lost an hour ago. You can win; now set about him.

After two more rounds great commotion prevailed in the midst of which Baldock and Donnelly looked very much like engaging in a scrap; but fortunately their men required carrying to their corners and the turmoil ceased.

Harper—Look at that eye, Jem, I'll give you my word he can't see you.

Kilrain (to Harper)—Yes, I can, and you, also, my gentleman.

When seven more rounds had been fought and the men were on the ground Kilrain, in answer to the cries of Smith's seconds to get off their man, said:

"IF I CAN'T WIN FAIR, I DON'T WANT TO WIN."

Mitchell—Smith has said he hoped Jake would make him fight half an hour. He'll be accommodated to-day.

At the termination of the 71st round Donnelly, while carrying Kilrain to his corner, sang "Sweet Violets." On completing 77 rounds Mitchell appealed to the referee, declaring that his man's face had been torn.

Smith—No, no; I wouldn't do such a thing.

Baldock—It isn't likely.

Mitchell—Oh! your god is a wooden one.

Kilrain, after showing his face to the referee and asking that official to "watch those fellows," walked to his corner and was subsequently ordered by Mitchell to make his time.

Harper—Wait till you meet Sullivan.

Mitchell—Ah! the sooner the better. I have beaten all comers, and when I meet that bluff the fight will not last so long as this. Be careful in that corner and don't try to break my man's fingers.

Harper—Smith's will break his jaw.

Fleming—The men are all right; it's the seconds who are making all the row.

Mitchell—Look out for Jack Baldock.

Baldock—You are a nice 'un; you'll want me to second you against Sullivan.

Mitchell (hearing some talk about postponement through darkness)—Say, don't talk about darkness; look at the moon. God bless the old moon.

A spectator—You'll want candles soon.

Concluding the 79th round, Smith's seconds attempted to carry him, but Jem said, "Let me walk."

Mitchell—Now, look here; there must be no nonsense this time or there'll be somebody hurt, and it won't be me.

As they advanced for the 101st round Mitchell said: "Now, let's have one good round and give the fight to the best man."

SOME OF SMITH'S TRICKS.

Then began a series of knock-down blows. Up to the 50th round Kilrain knocked Smith down twenty times. Smith's backers walked away from the ring. The men had been fighting steadily for more than an hour, and Smith was still facing the music. Then began the trouble that the handful of Americans had feared. Smith tried to gouge out Kilrain's eye. In one round later his second tried the same trick. In both cases the outrage was so plain that everybody saw it, and it should be said that it drove several Englishmen over to Kilrain's side. His magnificent fighting qualities commanded the admiration of even the heaviest losers, but there was a rowdy element that endorsed the tricky Briton. It was evident Smith was fighting for time. He would fall when Kilrain struck at him so as to gain time. Everything was done so as to stretch out the time.

Mitchell saw the scheme and protested hotly. He fought like a major, but the combination was too strong for him.

After the men had been fighting two hours and a half, and when Kilrain had brought the 106th round to a close by knocking Smith down and a left-handed blow in the jaw, the fight was declared a draw on account of darkness.

Kilrain was the lion on the trip home. He was so straight, manly and honest that the crowd forsook Smith and turned to the man who had fought so pluckily and fairly against long odds. Kilrain will come out well ahead, as Mr. Fox agreed to give him whatever money was up, win or lose.

The men are to fight again in a room with twelve people on a side to decide the championship. Already the betting is two to one on K.Irain.

After the fight the weary sportsmen trooped off by twos and threes to talk over the result of the match and avoid the police, who had become alert. If it had not been for Mitchell's persistent and belligerent espousal of Kilrain's cause there is no doubt that the American would have been very seriously maimed, if not blinded. It was to the credit of the Englishmen present that they were loudest and most emphatic in condemnation of the cowardly methods employed by Smith's second. Baldock was very brutal and atrocious in his efforts to make Smith win by foul play. At the Aquarium on Saturday, Dec. 10, at Sullivan's last exhibition, he said in the presence of several witnesses, "Yes, Smith will win. I would make him win if he were nothing but a cat."

The seconds were compelled to remain outside the ropes as long as the men were fighting, but the instant they clinched and went down the seconds jumped into the ring to lift them and carry them to their corners. It was at these moments that Baldock indulged in his foul practices. His agility was wonderful; he would spring over the ropes like a cat and throw himself upon the heels of the two pugilists with their bloody arms clasped around each other's necks. There would be a shout from Mitchell and very often from the spectators too, who observed the villainy of the second.

GOUGING KILRAIN'S EYE.

At the end of the 32d round, after Kilrain had staggered to his feet half blinded to the place where Atkinson, the referee, stood against the ropes, he pointed one finger to his left eye and said quietly:

"Mr. Atkinson, that man Baldock rammed his finger into my eye as I lay there and tried to gouge it out. You can see for yourself."

He was pointing to his left eye, from which the blood was streaming. The right eye had been closed for an hour. The wound in the eye was on the lower lid, where the nails of Smith's second had dug into it. Fortunately he had not succeeded in piercing the eye-ball. At this moment the two seconds of Smith were carrying that brawny but breathless champion of England to his corner. Atkinson reproved Baldock, and Kilrain went back to his corner.

In the thirty-eighth round the two men fell very near Smith's corner. Mitchell was on the other side of the 24-foot ring. Baldock was immediately over the spot where they lay. He vaulted the ropes and leaned over the men as though endeavoring to part them. In reality he seized one of Kilrain's fingers with the intention of breaking it. Mitchell's eye caught the motion, and he dashed across the ring landing on Baldock. The spectacle followed of a light-weight second flying at a large and muscular body. Mitchell struck Baldock in every way as he rushed at him, and knocked him completely out of the ring. Baldock, who certainly has plenty of pluck, came back over the ropes and rushed at Mitchell, livid and stuttering with rage. The other seconds separated them, and saved Baldock from what he deserved.

JAMES SMITH,
OF LONDON, ENG., THE CHAMPION PUGILIST OF GREAT BRITAIN.

AFTER THE BATTLE.

LONDON, Dec. 21, 1887.

Smith was gossiping with Howes and Roberts, his backers. He said: "They say Jake can't hit hard. All I can say is let 'em try it. That blow on the ear bothered me a lot, because, you see, it was done so early in the fight. They say Kilrain can't fight. Let 'em have a fight with him. He fights better than he spars.

"I feel first class. I have plenty of bruises about me, and one over the chest is like a breastplate. When I cough it hurts me. I could not see properly for three-quarters of an hour after the punch on the ear. That fellow has a good right hand. I hear Kilrain cannot get out of his bed.

"I was getting stronger during the last 6 rounds and felt wonderfully well."

KILRAIN CHEERFUL BUT BRUISED.

Kilrain, on arriving in London, went to Moore's house, in Finchley road, with Charley Mitchell. He was extremely cheerful. The external marks of punishment are an inflamed right eye, discoloration of the left optic and an abrasion over the forehead and nose. His hands are quite sound, and in every other respect his condition is as perfect as possible.

Kilrain said:—"I was up the next morning at half-past seven and had a bath. After breakfast, with Mitchell and Charley Rowell, I took a hack and rode up the Champs Elysee, through the Arc de Triomphe, into the Bois de Boulogne, on to the Autcuille Racecourse. Returning, we visited Napoleon's tomb, Notre Dame and the Morgue. We left Paris at a quarter to eight for London and arrived at Charing Cross at ten minutes past six."

THE PART MITCHELL PLAYED.

Mitchell then struck in about the absence of the American contingent, and said:

"Everything I could do to get them to the fight was done, so far as I was personally concerned. I went round for them the morning of the fight to their hotel. They did not come. I drove a second time to their hotel with Mr. Wm. E. Harding, but we could not find them. We were told that they had gone to the station. We were only just in time to catch the train which we nearly lost through looking for them. If they had an interest in their countryman winning and did not come to England from selfish motives, they could not expect me to leave my man on the day of the fight and look after anybody. I think I have proved to the sporting world at large that I did everything a man could do to bring Jake fit and well to the scratch. Having perfectly satisfied Kilrain, I feel more than satisfied with myself, as deeds speak for themselves."

KILRAIN FELT HURT.

Kilrain—For my part I felt hurt that they were not with me, as they are countrymen of mine. Mitchell made every effort to delay the fight in order to give them time to reach the rendezvous; but the determination to fight compelled me to make instantaneous arrangements, and the battle proceeded.

"I hope the members of the press are perfectly satisfied with the arrangements made for their accommodation, and trust they will treat us as we have treated them. From the present outlook pugilism is on the rise, and we shall have many more champion-ship fights in the near future.

KILRAIN IGNORES SULLIVAN.

"In regard to Sullivan's challenges I think it all a bluff. I ignore the challenge, also the challenger, as it is well known throughout the world that he has refused to fight me. My money was up for three months, and by refusing to meet me he forfeited any pretensions he might have had to championship honors, but should it go wrong with Charley I'll fight him as soon as he likes and for as much as he likes. But there, let the matter drop. He will not beat Charley, and as a natural consequence my desire to meet him will not be gratified.

HIS OPINION OF SMITH.

"Smith is undoubtedly a good, game man, and having met him in battle I shall be pleased to meet him in friendship. As to the treatment I received at the hands of the

English public, I can't find words to sufficiently express my gratitude. All over the country my reception has been princely, and wherever I have gone kindly words have been said and the best of wishes expressed for my welfare to the end of my days, and when I'm far away from England recollection of this visit will crowd out from my memory all the remaining acts of kindness tendered to me away from my home.

GRATITUDE TO ROWELL AND HARDING.

"I must not forget to say a word in Charley Rowell's favor. He was my guide, philosopher and friend all through my training and conscientiously looked after my interest to the bitter end."

Mitchell—Jake, we must make Harding a little present. What is it to be?

Kilrain—Whatever he likes—with all my heart.

Mitchell—Well, he hasn't got a diamond ring, so we will give him one and present it on the stage of the Washington Music Hall next Saturday evening. It will be a present from myself.

THE MEN IN PARIS.

PARIS, Dec. 20.

From a special to POLICE GAZETTE.

When the glorious sun broke through the window of the Hotel de l'Athenee this morning it discovered a tableau that for a moment caused it to waver and grow dim, as though obscured by a passing cloud. The spectacle in question was located on the second floor. Two tubs were placed within a foot of each other, and in them sat two mighty gladiators paddling water gently with their scarred and swollen fists and glancing at each other's billowy muscles.

Yesterday Smith and Kilrain were fighting as though for their lives. To-day their names were in the world's mouth. Even the French newspapers have gone agog over the great contest, the universal feeling here in Paris being that it is a triumph of nineteenth century civilization that two men could meet in the presence of members of the French and English nobility and pummel each other without losing temper or presence of mind. Nothing could have exceeded the friendly feeling that the two battered pugilists exhibited this morning.

"That's a terrible left you've got there, Jem," remarked Kilrain, looking with undisguised admiration at the Englishman's big arm, "'twas that loosened my ear."

"No, Jack," corrected the other, allowing water to drip slowly over the big arm on to his shoulder, "I done that with my right. It was after the fifth round when you slipped sideways."

"Well, do you know what it was?" asked Kilrain, slowly but earnestly. "It was a soaker."

At this gracious and magnanimous praise an expression of conscious embarrassment came over the battered assortment of rumpled features that Mr. Smith is wearing in lieu of what was formerly his face. But while he realized that the compliment was deserved, he felt that it was too much to accept without some return, so he raised his big and now irregular hand to his own ear, and remarked quietly:

"Well, this here clip of yours was felt by me at the time."

Kilrain looked half diffidently down into the water. This was high praise from the champion of England. Personally I think it was deserved, for I remember that when the blow fell it caused Mr. Smith to reel over and drop to the earth. Ten minutes later the whole ear had swollen to the size of a big pear. It was lanced afterward.

The men enjoyed their baths. It was the first chance they had had to look each other over. The minute the fight was finished they were helped to their quarters on the tug and plied with champagne. They had been in strict training for months and months and wine tasted good to them. Sensibly enough, their seconds allowed them to have all they could drink. "Let them get loaded, if they want to," said Mitchell. He said no two men ever did a harder day's work, and they deserved a little reward. The pugilists had all they could drink, and they were thirsty when they arrived at Paris. They were as happy as lords. After their many wounds were dressed they were put to bed, and they did not meet again till this morning, when they sat in rival tubs and looked each other over with the conversation described.

Kilrain talked very freely to his friends about the mill. "It makes a big difference," he said, "in a fight, whether you have on hand friends yelling for you or a hundred enemies yelling against you. I went there to win and did my best, but I might have done a little stronger work if I'd a bigger crowd behind me at the start. But the spectators treated me well after the mill. They did, indeed. Lots of English gents came up to me afterward and said they were with me and glad I did so well."

JEM SMITH'S COLORS.

[FROM THE POLICE GAZETTE, JAN. 28, 1888.]

JAKE KILRAIN, CHAMPION OF THE WORLD, RECEIVES $6,000 IN COLD CASH

—HE VISITS DUBLIN—LONDON "PUNCH" WISHES A HAPPY NEW 'EAR

TO JEM SMITH—KILRAIN AND SMITH AT THE AQUARIUM—SULLIVAN'S

BLUSTER.

The curtain descended on the final act of the international prize fight between Jem Smith and Jake Kilrain, the champions of the Old and New Worlds at the *Sporting Life* office yesterday. At 2 P. M. Jake Kilrain with Charley Mitchell, each attired in fur-lined top coats, trimmed with sealskin, drove up to the *Sporting Life* office, where they had agreed to meet Mr. William E. Harding, Mr. Richard K. Fox's representative, to draw the stake money. Richard K. Fox posted on behalf of Kilrain for his match with Smith, in addition to the £200 given by Mr. Richard K. Fox's representative to Kilrain to bet in the ring. A large crowd assembled in Fleet street so soon as it was whispered that Kilrain (the American champion, and holder of the "Police Gazette" diamond belt, representing the championship of the world) had arrived, and intense excitement prevailed.

Charley Mitchell soon broached the business. "Well," he said, "we have come to draw the stakes Mr. Richard K. Fox put up for Jake's match with Smith."

Harding—I have just received a cable from Mr. Fox desiring me to issue a challenge through the *Sporting Life* to the effect that he is anxious to back Kilrain against John L. Sullivan, to fight in the United States or Mexico, in six months, according to the rules of the London prize ring, for the "Police Gazette" diamond belt and the championship of the world, Mr. Fox to stake $15,000 on Kilrain against $10,000.

Kilrain—I will fight Sullivan any time he is ready to make a bona fide match, but I will not allow Mr. Richard K. Fox (my backer) to lay odds. Sullivan has got a match on now, and it may be that he will find his hands full. If Mitchell beats him then I do not want to fight Sullivan.

Mitchell—I give you my word I feel confident of beating Sullivan.

Harding—You will not do anything of the kind. Bull is final stakeholder and appears to be backing Sullivan. I believe it was his £100 posted on the night the match was made, so what show have you got?

Mitchell—You will find out on the day of the fight. I never could get Sullivan to fight me in America. I fought him when I only weighed 10. stone 3 pounds, and he weighed 14 stone. I floored him with a square knock-down blow, and fiddled him all over the ring, and would have beaten him sure had not the police stepped in and spoiled the business.

Kilrain—One thing I do know. Mr. Richard K. Fox put up $1,000 forfeit for me to fight Sullivan for $5,000 a side and the "Police Gazette" diamond belt, and the big fellow failed to cover the money.

Harding—Say, Kilrain, I will now draw out a formal receipt, which you can sign. You must also give the *Sporting Life* one, and then you will receive your stake money. This, with the £200 I handed to you in the ring, makes £1,200 ($6,000). Let me tell you it is more money than John L. Sullivan received when he fought Paddy Ryan for the championship of America.

Mitchell—Is that so?

Kilrain—Yes; Sullivan only fought for $2,500.

Harding then drew up an acknowledgement, which Jake immediately signed.

The American champion was then handed a check for his stake money by Mr. George W. Atkinson, of the *Sporting Life*, and the party adjourned to Anderson's Hotel, where, presided over by Messrs. Clemow, sparkling wine was imbibed. Kilrain and Mitchell drove off in a well-appointed buggy, cheered by a large and enthusiastic crowd. —*London Sporting Life, Dec.* 29.

KILRAIN IN DUBLIN.

DUBLIN, Jan. 6, 1888.

Kilrain and Mitchell arrived at Waterford this morning by the Milford boat. Kilrain, referring to Burke's challenge, said that he would go to Australia if he got $500 for expenses. He is of the opinion that Burke does not want to fight, but he is anxious only to get home.

The pugilists were entertained at luncheon by Mr. Manning, and large crowds collected for the purpose of getting a peep at them.   They left Waterford at half-past two o'clock.

At Maryboro several sporting gentlemen met Kilrain and produced a cablegram from Mr. Fox, expressing pride in Kilrain's fight with the British champion, and adding : "Tell Jake when you meet him I'll back him to fight John L. Sullivan or any other man in the world for $10,000." Kilrain was well pleased with this fresh evidence of his backer's appreciation.

At Kingsbridge station, Dublin, the Kilrain party were met by a large crowd of friends and admirers, who were astonished to find that the great battle than a trifling bloodshot eye.   They were driven to the Grosvenor Hotel, where they will sojourn during their visit to Dublin.

It is stated that Mitchell will shortly go into training for the Sullivan fight.   John L. goes into training quarters next Friday.

There was an enormous crush at the Star Music Hall this evening.   Long before the hour for commencing, the house, which is rather small, was crammed from floor to ceiling and the doors were closed on an enormous crowd outside awaiting the arrival of the pugilists.   There was no one of prominence among the audience.

Kilrain and Mitchell appeared on the stage at a quarter past 9 o'clock, receiving a great ovation.   There was no speechmaking, and they at once went to business.

They fought three two-minute rounds.   Both drew forth frequent applause by clever stopping and getting away.—*Herald Correspondent.*

KILRAIN AND SMITH BOX AT THE AQUARIUM.

[FROM SPECIAL TO POLICE GAZETTE.]

LONDON, Jan. 10, 1888.

An immense audience at increased prices gathered, and among it were a large number of feminine lovers of nerve and muscle—"the fistic," as one Amazon in crimson plush from boots to bonnet phrased it.   The contest was, of course, the same as when the two men were in the ring exactly two weeks ago.   The American was the greatest object of curiosity, for Smith is something of a chestnut.

Mr. Fleming introduced the twain in a speech, and then their there rounds began. Directly the men faced each other Kilrain led off with the left, but was neatly countered.   He then got one in for nothing which Smith afterward followed up by a substantial body blow.   Both men used the left with precision, and some sneezers were put in which called forth plaudits and "Bravo, Kilrain !"   "Good, old Jem !"

In the second round some heavy digs were given and received, and the sparring scientific honors seemed equally divided.   In the third round Kilrain again led off, but Smith was on his trail and a give-and-take bout of a heavy character was carried on from start to finish, after which they received a very hearty recall.

They showed few signs of the ordeal recently passed through.   Smith's ear is a trifle thick yet, reminding one of *Punch's* last week's wish to him—"A Happy New 'ear."

They each receive £1,000 for twelve nights, and a percentage of the receipts also beyond £100 per night in the provinces.

SMITH FAILS TO MEET SULLIVAN.

LONDON, Jan. 11.

Since his arrival in this land, Sullivan, the pride of Boston and the boast of America, has planted admiration, awe and respect in every heart, and these things have been placed especially deep in the hearts of the police who have to run this big town.   The first time he came they took it calmly.   Thousands of delighted admirers turned out, walked over the few police who got together, and taught the entire force such a lesson that they have never made the mistake since.   To-day, for instance, a small paragraph appeared saying that the great and only Sullivan would be at the *Sportsman* office at 2 o'clock.   Long before that time the police were on hand in force sufficient to handle a riot or anything that might turn up.   They were wise for they were needed.

Fleet street once more was jammed.   Thousands of Londoners abandoned all business to have a look at the great man who was to come, and stood yelling and shouting

WILLIAM E. HARDING, OF NEW YORK,
SPORTING EDITOR OF THE "POLICE GAZETTE" AND RICHARD K. FOX'S REPRESENT-
ATIVE IN THE INTERNATIONAL PRIZE FIGHT BETWEEN KILRAIN AND SMITH.

while 'busses, cabs and a funeral piled thems-lves in picturesque chaos for blocks in every direction. Sullivan, with wisdom, entered the office by a roundabout way. He had come according to announcement with friends and money ready, in his own vigorous and not self-deprecating words. to "lick any man, at any time, for any amount." The challenge was extended to all fighters of class No. 2, Sullivan alone being in class No. 1.

Smith, &c., had shown a good deal of wisdom of a negative sort. They were not on hand. Not one of them wants to fight, and so they did not come.

For a long time Sullivan bewailed his lot in tones deep and mixed with profanity. He had a new and startling epithet for every one of the alleged fighters, and not one of them would have been pleased with the remark that was chosen for him, though each remark had a rough element of justice in it. It was in vain for Sullivan's friends to seek to soothe him. He would not be soothed, and did not even take his friends' efforts kindly. The fact which preys especially upon the soul of the world's champion fighter is that the excuse of men afraid of him is that he must first fight Mitchell. Sullivan declines to look on his engagement with Mitchell as a fight. He considers it simply as an undertaking on his part to knock Mitchell senseless if, when the time comes, he shall be foolhardy enough to go into a ring, which is extremely doubtful.

Mitchell, by the way, is in for an unpleasant time if he does fight, according to Jack Ashton, who spars with Sullivan, and is for that good reason his devoted admirer. "The big fellow," said Ashton, "is dead sore on Mitchell, and he'll make Mitchell know it. They talk about Mitchell being knocked out right away, but worse than that is waiting for him. The big fellow won't knock him out right away if he can possibly help it. He wants to hurt Mitchell for all the lying he has done about him, and he'll go for his ribs and heart and keep away from his neck and chin and knock-out blows. Mitchell, of course, is hoping that the big fellow will take to drinking and give him a chance, but he'll have no such luck. If he ever goes up against the big fellow he'll get that old right pounding on to his insides, and he won't want any more fight for a long time, nor be the same fighting man if he wanted to."

Sullivan, who heard Ashton's remarks, smiled gleefully for a moment as he fondly weighed his right fist in his left, but then gloom spread over his features once more as he expressed mournfully the conviction that Mitchell would keep his heart out of reach of his (Sullivan's) right.

After an hour's waiting nobody had come to accept the champion's offer to fight, and meanwhile policemen had been coming up at intervals, haggard, but deferential, to tell Sullivan that they could not get the crowd away, and that he really must do something. Sullivan concluded that the best thing to do was to go away. He put his head out of the window and bowed with politeness and condescension to his delighted admirers. The crowd assured Sullivan that he could beat them all, and sarcastically commented on the significant absence of all the other fighters. This display of friendship reached Sullivan's heart, under its many layers of muscle, and he said, like a king or any other man of that class:

"I'll go down and give them a chance to see me."

So he went down, and hundreds who could get near him cheered, squeezed each other's breath out and proved plainly that they were happy. Many in their delight patted him on the back, and not less than ten delighted mortals were shaking each of his hands. All the while Sullivan, who loves his popularity dearly, smiled blissfully and enjoyed himself. An ordinary man would have risked broken bones or worse in such a crowd, but Sullivan is not ordinary. He went placidly through the crowd as a steam shovel goes through the snow, and was not disturbed by the human waves dashing against his new blue overcoat. At last he got into a cab and drove away, but it was not easy, for the crowd surging ahead of him, drove cabs and all before it, and even the plucky cabman, who had determined to win a shilling and glory by taking the great fighter, in spite of his efforts to knock down his fellow-citizens, was pushed back almost a block before Sullivan could reach him.

When the cab was under way it was surrounded still with scrambling. yelling hundreds, and in this triumphant fashion Sullivan disappeared from view. He was bound for Chippy Norton's place, at Windsor. There he will breathe ozone, exercise, eat and get ready for work, should any one turn up. He is absolutely sober, and has been so ever since his arrival. For a week he has not smoked, and he will continue to abstain from tobacco. All his joys are gone. When asked how he managed to stand it he smiled, not cheerfully, and said, in his deepest tones:

"Somebody will have to pay me back for leading a Sunday school superintendent's life, and if I can't get at any one else, Mitchell will have to foot the whole bill."

Who would be Mitchell? Sullivan looks much thinner and better. His mustache is grown in this damp climate, and has taken to curling, let us hope of its own accord.

THE EMBLEM OF THE WORLD'S CHAMPIONSHIP.

The "Police Gazette" diamond belt, which is the heavy-weight championship trophy of the prize ring, in value and artistic excellence outranks anything of the kind ever manufactured, and will, no doubt, in time become as famous as the cherished relic which so many of the heroes of the ring pluckily fought for in merry England.

It will for all time be a certificate of manly valor and physical culture and skill to any fortunate enough to wear it. The belt that the proprietor of the POLICE GAZETTE. New York, offers for competition for the championship fighters of the world is wel worthy of the purpose, and is itself entitled to the name of champion of the world as a "belt." It is 50 inches long and 8 inches wide, and weighs about 200 ounces in solid silver and gold. The design of this marvelous work of art is entirely different from any prize belt that was ever offered in this country or in Europe, and, in intrinsic value has never been equaled. The work is laid out by solid silver plates and flexible woven silver chains, fortunately, so that the belt, notwithstanding its great and ponderous weight and size, can be adjusted to the body and worn with ease. The plates are richly ornamented with solid gold figures, and one of these ornaments is so made that the likeness of the winner can be put in a gold frame encircled by a solid gold laurel wreath suspended from the bill of a full-winged eagle. The centre of the belt represents a prize ring with two men facing each other in fighting attitude. The whole of this part is solid gold. The men are represented in full ring costume. The prize ring is encircled by eight large diamonds, and the top of it ornamented with a fox's head emblematical of the donor, Richard K. Fox, with diamond eyes.

The champion belt of England, which John Carmel Heenan of Troy, N. Y., better known as the Benecia Boy, and Tom Sayers of London, England, the respective champions of England and America in 1859 and 1860, fought for was a historical and valuable trophy, but it was not half as costly as the "Police Gazette" diamond belt Jem Smith and Jake Kilrain did battle for.

THE RULES WHICH GOVERNED THE FIGHT.

RULE 1—The "Police Gazette" diamond belt shall represent the heavy-weigh championship of the world, and be open for every man to compete for.

RULE 2—All contests for the "Police Gazette" diamond belt shall be fought ac cording to the new rules of the London prize ring and the "Police Gazette" rules, op tional with the men arranging the contest.

RULE 3—The holder of the trophy will be the recognized champion pugilist of th world, and will be required to defend the trophy against all comers.

RULE 4—All matches for the belt shall be for no less a sum than one thousand do lars ($1,000) a side or upward, at the option of the holder.

RULE 5—The belt shall be subject to challenge from any pugilist in the world, bu no challenge will be accepted unless a deposit of $250 is posted with the office of th POLICE GAZETTE.

RULE 6—Challenges shall date from the day of their receipt by the stakeholder, an the holder of the belt shall be in duty bound to arrange a match with the first chr lenger.

RULE 7—All contests shall take place within three months or sooner, if option with the holder, from the date of receipt of challenge by the stakeholder.

RULE 8—The holder of the belt must contend for the belt every four months, challenged, and not more than three times in twelve months.

RULE 9—In all matches for the "Police Gazette" diamond belt the donor shall stakeholder, and his representative must be present at every contest for the trophy order to settle any dispute in question that may arise in regard to the rules.

RULE 10 –The donor of the belt shall also, if optional with the principals, select t battle ground and act as or appoint the referee.

RULE 11—In all contests for the "Police Gazette" diamond belt the donor or h representative shall settle all disputes in regard to time of weighing and in the sele tion of the battle ground.

RULE 12—In case of magisterial interference the referee, if appointed, if not, th stakeholder or his representative, shall select, name and notify both men of the ne, time and place of fighting.

RULE 13—All contests for the belt must be fought in the United States, Canada

CHARLEY MITCHELL,
FAMOUS PUGILIST, MANAGER, TRAINER, ETC., OF JAKE KILRAIN.

Europe, and the holder of the trophy will have no power to select the fighting ground, but will mutually agree with the challenger and holder upon the selection of the place.

RULE 14—If the holder of the belt and the challenger agree upon the place of meeting, the stakeholder will select the fighting ground.

RULE 15—The belt shall become the personal property of any pugilist who wins it three times in succession, or holds it three years against all comers.

RULE 16—The winner or holder of the belt must give satisfactory security for the safe keeping of the same, and be prompt to return it to the stakeholder when called for.

RULE 17—The belt must be delivered to the stakeholder thirty days prior to a contest, and the holder refusing any challenge will forfeit all claims and rights to the trophy.

RULE 18—The holder of the "Police Gazette" diamond belt shall be the recognized heavy-weight champion of the world.

PRESS COMMENTS ON THE DEPARTURE OF WILLIAM E. HARDING FOR ENGLAND.

New York Star, Nov. 13.—William E. Harding, the sporting editor of the POLICE GAZETTE, sailed for England on the Etruria yesterday, at 2 P. M. Col. Harding will represent Mr. Richard K. Fox on behalf of Kilrain in the great international championship fight with Jem Smith, at Madrid, Spain, on Jan. 3 next. He carries to Kilrain Mr. Fox's check for $1,000, which will be presented to Kilrain to bet on himself in the fight.

New York Daily News, Nov. 13.—William E. Harding, sporting editor of the *News* and POLICE GAZETTE, sailed for Europe yesterday, on the Etruria. Hundreds of his friends assembled to see him off, and many of them sent him baskets of flowers. Mr. Harding goes abroad as the representative of Richard K. Fox in the international prize fight between Kilrain and Smith, which will take place in Spain in January. Mr. Fox has brought the champions of America and England so far toward the contest with eminent success. This is the first representative international contest for many years, and if it is concluded by a battle it will be the first one of the kind since Heenan and Sayers met. So far it has cost about $10,000 of Mr. Fox's money, including the belt, Kilrain's expenses, stakes, etc. Mr. Harding yesterday had a draft on London for £200 ($1,000) indorsed, "to be handed to Jake Kilrain in the ring to bet upon the result, and be his if he wins." On his arrival in London he will make the *Sporting Life* office his headquarters.

New York Sun, Nov. 13.—William Gammon, the Park Row jeweler, sent to William E. Harding of the POLICE GAZETTE, at his office on Saturday morning a handsome solid silver gold-lined coffee set. Each piece bears the inscription : "William E. Harding, compliments William Gammon."

New York Sun, Nov. 15.—William E. Harding has been sent with £200 to present Jake Kilrain when he steps into the ring to fight Jem Smith. Harding sailed on the Etruria on Saturday.

William E. Harding, the sporting editor of the POLICE GAZETTE, sailed for England Nov. 12, on the Etruria, of the Cunard line. He has gone abroad as the representative of Mr. Richard K. Fox, and carries that gentleman's check for $1,000, which will be given Kilrain to bet on himself when he enters the ring. He will look after the American champion's (Kilrain's) interest in the great international fight of Jan. 3 next, at Madrid, Spain, for the "Police Gazette" diamond belt and $10,000 in stakes.

John Wood, Police Captain Webb, Jere Dunn, John Charles, of Baltimore, Richard K. Fox, Oakey Kerker, Frank Stevenson, Andy Kelly, Billy Dacey, Johnny Reagan, Mark Maguire of the *Sun,* Ned Plummer of the *Star,* George Bartholomew, editor of the *Daily News,* were among the many friends who saw him off. Many handsome presents were sent him. The floral emblems were many and rich. A handsome horseshoe came from Richard K. Fox. Wm. Gammon, the Park Row jeweler, sent to the POLICE GAZETTE office in the morning a handsome solid silver, gold-lined, coffee set; each piece bears the inscription : "Wm. E. Harding, compliments Wm. Gammon."

The *Sporting Life,* of London, where the $10,000 stakes are held, will be the headquarters of Harding. His immediate care will be the looking after the welfare of Kilrain. The final arrangements for the fight will be completed at once. John Fleming will act for Smith. The stakes complete are now in the possession of the *Sporting Life,* London ; $8,000 was posted at that office and the first $2,000 with the New York *Clipper;*

this amount, which was forwarded to London on Oct. 24, has been received and acknowledged as follows: ·

Yesterday (Friday) we received a draft for $2,000 on the Union Bank, London, and the following letter:

> *The New York Clipper,*
> 88 and 90 Centre St. New York, October 24, 1887.
>
> *" To the Editor of the " Sporting Life ":*
>
> SIR—Enclosed find a draft covering the amount posted at this office for the Smith-Kilrain match. Said amount (2,000 dols.) we turn over to the *Sporting Life,* permanent stakeholder. Yours, &c.,   G. W. KEIL.
>
> The Frank Queen Publishing Company (Limited).
> —*Sporting Life,* Nov. 5.

Nothing now remains to be done but to select the battle ground. In this every precaution will be taken to select a place remote from interference by the authorities and that the toughs cannot reach. Both men went into training last week. Kilrain is a hard and earnest worker; he has never been dissipated, and with the clever and experienced Charley Mitchell to work with him, he will be in the best condition of his life for the fight, and will enter the ring with $1,000 of Richard K. Fox's in his hands, given him to bet that he will win.

* * *

OFFICIAL REPORT OF THE FIGHT.

After the ring had been pitched upon it, all disembarked, and prepared for the fray. The company included many well-known racing men. Among them were Messrs. Homer, Harlow, Byron Weber, Blakeley Hall, W. Wilde, J. H.Smith, Jr., Archibald Allison, W. Plummer, R. Watson, Archibald McNeil, Henry Heyney, Frank Hinde, Capt. Lee-Barber, Col. Browne, Capt. Grenville, Arthur Coventry, Aubrey Coventry, Lord De Clifford, Capt. Jones, Mr. Jones, Lord Mayo, Capt. Price, the Hon. Michael Sandys, J. O'Neil, Arthur Cooper, Alf Saville, Marquis Queensberry, Mr. Carew, Lord Churston, Dan Armitage, John Percival, Tony Sage, Capt. A. Drummond, Mr. H. Drummond, W. Mackay, Poney Moore, F. Johnson, Johnny Gideon, Dan Gideon, W. Low, Ernest Wells (proprietor of the Pelican Club), S. Singard, Arthur Coburn, Capt. Bailey, E. C. Smith, Mr. Mededith, etc., etc.

It may be as well to repeat that Kilrain's staff were Charley Mitchell and Ned Donnelly, seconds; Charley Rowell, bottleholder; Mr. W. E. Harding (New York POLICE ＾AZETTE), timekeeper and umpire. Smith's were the two Jacks, Harper and Baldock; ⌐ick Roberts, bottle holder; Mr. J. Fleming, umpire and timekeeper. Mr. George W. Atkinson, of the *Sporting Life,* at the request of both sides, officiated as referee. The usual preparations went on in regard to choice of corners. There was no very great advantage, but Baldock beat Mitchell in tossing, and selected the higher ground, giving Smith also the sun at his back. The wind, which was very keen, came across the ring between the two camps, and the sun's line was almost straight from one corner to the other. Dick Roberts and Tom Smith pitched a first rate ring, and the usual collection was made.

ROUND 1—At the first call of time the men walked from their corners. Before a blow had been struck 3 to 1 was laid on Smith, and even as they came together 70 to 20 three or four times was laid on Smith, once by a well-known gentleman owner and most promising rider, who declared to win for Smith's benefit. Smith started by trying for the point with the left, which Kilrain stopped well enough, but directly afterward began sparring with his elbows out in a very awkward fashion. Both played cautiously to get each other's measure. After several tries Jem got his left on the cheek, and just missed a counter. Next time Smith went for the head with his left, and only just missed a hot right-hander, but was caught on the ribs with the left before he completely recovered himself. Smith let go the left, followed with the right, but no harm had been done when he and Kilrain came down, Smith under. Time, 35 seconds.

ROUND 2—As Kilrain sat in his corner his old-fashioned face wore a grim smile, while Smith appeared as if he was quite satisfied with his first feeler at the American, although the latter had a little the best of the deal. The pair came up quickly to the call of "Time!" Very little was done. They led off almost simultaneously. Each got home on the cheek with the left, and then closed. In the struggle for the fall Smith came to the top as they reached the ground. Time, 12 seconds.

JOHN PERCIVAL, SMITH'S BACKER.

DAN M'CANNON, SMITH'S OLD SECOND.

CHARLES WHITE, "THE DUKE'S MOTTO."

Round 3—Smith was quicker to start, landing at the chin, and stopped Kilrain's counter. Kilrain sent his left at the belly, but Smith made up by placing his left on the American's mouth. Kilrain led, and just reached the forehead, and then got a warm one right on the ribs, for which Smith paid him with his left on the jaw. They closed and came down locked.

Round 4—Both were blowing a little as they left their corners. Smith scored with a straight drive on the mouth. After this they sparred lightly. Kilrain led off and reached Smith's jaw. The Englishman scored with the left on the mouth, but Kilrain countered on the neck. At close quarters some heavy exchanges ensued. Ultimately they got into holds, and several hard tussels ensued for the fall. As usual, they were holding very tightly when they fell, Smith under. Time, 21 seconds.

Round 5—Kilrain came up with a very determined look and led off, but the blow was dodged by Smith. Kilrain next vainly tried to wrestle with his man. Before anything worth mentioning had been done the two closed holds and went down. This round lasted 14 seconds. [The previous rounds had all of them been short. The ground had by this time worn down a good deal on the side on the left of Smith's corner; the grass which had been long at the start, was trodden in. All the work had been done in a strip not one-third the width of the ring. In each bout, on the call of "Time!" Smith advanced to rather beyond midway between the two corners, and there showed disposition to lead at Kilrain. After that Kilrain worked to his right hand side, and Smith almost always kept to his left. To anticipate, at the end of the 2 hours and 31 minutes fighting, there was hardly a footmark, the one-half of the ring being divided diagonally between the corners.] Before "Time" was called for

Round 6—Kilrain's hands were dressed with ground resin, an example shortly followed in Smith's corner. When Smith led this time at Kilrain he got on the jaw, but only slightly, and stopped Kilrain's low counter. Then the American got home one on the ribs, and next, after a wait, Smith crossed the American with the right. At that Kilrain rushed in, and each scored two or three times on the body before they commenced hugging. Smith was down first, but was laughing as Harper and Baldock carried him to his corner. At this time 4 to 1 was laid on Smith.

Round 7—Smith, at the call of "Time" crossed over to Kilrain's corner and called to him to come out. Smith sent a warm one in on the chest, which was paid with a very hot one on the ribs with the ponderous right hand. On this Smith drew in, and after a short rally closed with the American, and they ended with the usual wrestle. Time, 21 seconds.

Round 8—The first seven rounds had occupied eight minutes. Smith waited for Kilrain to lead, but did not time him correctly. When the American did commence business he got home on Smith's right temple. Twice Smith essayed to reach his opponent's head, but failed. Kilrain got in two heavy blows with his right in rapid succession. They closed, and Smith was ultimately back-heeled. Time, 19 seconds.

Round 9—Smith came up cheerfully. Kilrain led off on the forehead, and then Smith answered with a straight one on the chest, but was smartly countered : then the usual wrestle ensued. Time, 18 seconds.

Round 10—So soon as Smith began he fairly bustled the American, and landed three or four times on the ribs with both hands. Then Jake woke up, and sent in a rare drive on the cheek with his right. It was answered by Smith with a straight 'un on the cheek. The round finished in Smith's corner, he falling against the stake.

Round 11—Neither so anxious to begin this time, and they sparred for some seconds prior to drawing to close quarters. At length Kilrain found an opening, and sent in his right very heavily on the Englishman's ribs, following it up with a straight left on the jaw. Then Smith scored a splendid straight drive on the chest, which he followed up with a couple of half-arm digs with the right. Kilrain then closed, and the customary finish came with a dog fall. Time, 32 seconds.

Round 12—On leaving their corners both were blowing a bit, the Englishman most perhaps. The round finished by Smith being thrown. Time, 14 seconds.

Round 13—At this point the weather turned piercingly cold. Smith made a play at the outset, but Kilrain landed right and left on his ribs. Then Jem very cleverly landed one-two on each side of the face, but he was more than lucky to stop a tremendous punch from Kilrain's left. So far there had been rather too much wrestling. Time, 16 seconds.

Round 14—Even. Time, 23 seconds.

Round 15—Smith started with his left, while Kilrain got in a rare pile driver with the left on the mark. Next Smith landed a grand one on the nose, which Jake wiped off with a smart left on the chest. Smith went for his man with a great deal of fire, and had the best of the fall. Time, 53 seconds.

Round 16—After an objection to the fact of Smith's seconds pulling their man into his corner had been overruled, Kilrain led off as before, but was cleverly stopped at the next attempt, Smith countering him on the mouth, and following up with a swinging right-hander that fairly staggered his opponent, Kilrain laid himself open for another, but Smith declined the invitation, and both went down in a scrambling fall. Time, 33 seconds.

ROUND 17—When the men again faced each other it was evident that Kilrain was in the better condition of the pair, as Jem was blowing while his opponent would hardly have puffed out a candle, his mouth being firmly closed. Smith dodged for an opening, but Kilrain was equal to the occasion, and, after feinting, let go his right with terrific force, knocking Smith clean off his legs. The sound of the blow could have been heard fifty yards away. Time, 7 seconds.

ROUND 18—Kilrain forcing the fighting. Smith, pulling himself together, fairly surprised his friends. Dodging the American's well-meant left, he clinched, and, fairly throwing him, walked back to his corner. Time, 12 seconds.

ROUND 19—Kilrain led off with his left on the point of the jaw, and then just missed his mark with a one-two. They then closed, and Kilrain, getting his left around Jem's neck attempted to put his head in chancery, but Jem cleverly extricated himself and slipped down. Time, 32 seconds.

ROUND 20—No more offers to lay odds on the Englishman were heard. Smith came up laughing, and landed his left well on the mark, but Kilrain, who had been waiting for an opening, at length shot out his right and sent Smith once more to the grass. Time, 29 seconds.

ROUND 21—Acting on the advice of Mitchell, who counseled Kilrain to go for his man, who had recovered his good-natured appearance after his knock-down in the last round, the American endeavored to follow up his success by letting go a well-meant left-hander, and stopped a heavy return from Jem. The latter then ducked under another of Kilrain's right-hander's, which brought about the usual struggle on the ropes, varied on this occasion, as while Smith laid himself out solely to throw Kilrain, the latter tried to disengage one hand to fib with, and after twice landing on Smith's ribs the pair came down. Time, 29 seconds.

ROUND 22—Smith came up with a smile, and Jake opened with the left on the shoulder, receiving in turn a stinging right-handed smack on the side of the head. Kilrain was under in the fall. This was a long round and a business one, and lasted 99 seconds.

ROUND 23—Matters were pretty equal. Time, 40 seconds.

ROUND 24—Kilrain sent the right straight out on the jaw—a regular staggerer. Smith pulled himself together in marvelous fashion, and bored in. The pair closed for the fall, and while they were struggling for the mastery Baldock cried out, "You can't throw him!" to which Jake replied, "Can't I?" and down Jem went. Time, 16 seconds.

ROUND 25—Smith once more came up as jauntily as circumstances would permit. After heavy exchanges Kilrain slipped up near his corner. Time, 21 seconds.

ROUND 26—Considering the pace at which they had been fighting, it was simply wonderful that so little visible damage had been effected.

ROUND 27.—This time Kilrain took the initiative, but he led short, an example too eagerly imitated by Jem, who, following the American up too far, was punished for his temerity by a slashing straght right-handed drive. Time, 27 seconds.

ROUND 28—Kilrain was again the aggressor, and got his left home on the point without a return, but Smith was quickly even with him, sending his left likewise on the point and his right flush on the face with telling effect. A fair give-and-take battle ensued, Kilrain landing twice with his left on the neck and ear. while Smith, coming at his man like a lion, drove his left right into his opponent's ribs, but just failed to follow up this success with the right. Two capital rallies succeeded. Jem placing his right prettily on the point, in response to which Kilrain again reached the damaged ear with his right, a blow which brought about a close, and a nasty fall for both, who were clinging tightly to each other's neck as they came down. Time, 29 seconds.

ROUND 29—This round ended harmlessly. Time, 21 seconds.

ROUND 30—Smith had the best of the fall. Time, 9 seconds.

ROUND 31—Both smart up to time. After a feint from Smith, Kilrain led, but only reached the neck, and Smith, countering in magnificent style, landed a grand swinging right-hand hit just below the ear. After a severe, sharp struggle they fell almost locked together. Time, 14 seconds.

ROUND 32—Mitchell claimed a foul on the ground that Baldock had attempted to gouge, but Mr. Atkinson ordered the men to fight on. Time, 32 seconds.

ROUND 33—Smith showed himself strongest in the wrestle, and finally threw Kilrain. Time, 23 seconds.

ROUND 34—Both were laughing when they fell. Time, 29 seconds.

ROUND 35—By this time it was evident to the spectators that unless some unforeseen accident should occur, this "battle of the giants" was likely to be a protracted one. It was simply marvellous to see the way in which the pair kept on their legs.

ARTHUR COOPER. SMITH'S BACKER.

JACK HARPER, SMITH'S SECOND.

J. HOWES, SMITH'S SECOND.

Smith began bustling about, but could hardly get home an effective blow, and not much done before Kilrain, in a scuffle, got in two or three light digs without a return. Time, 35 seconds.

ROUND 36—There could be no question that Smith had finished the last round much the stronger of the pair, and so it was not surprising to see him, after fairly coming up to the scratch, take the lead. His first effort was successful, as he landed a rare hot 'un with his left on Kilrain's ear, which bled freely for some time after. After a short struggle both went down. Time, 19 seconds.

ROUND 37—Smith was evidently the stronger of the pair, and his backers, seeing that he was still fresh, began to think the turning point had now been reached. Time, 26 seconds.

ROUND 38—Kilrain came up looking more determined than ever, but was met by Smith flush with the left. Jem, in following this advantage up, just failed to bring off a two-handed coup on the point. Kilrain, nothing daunted, bore Smith on to the ropes, where Jem went down. Time, 22 seconds.

ROUND 39—Smith was certainly the strongest of the pair.

ROUND 40 was a rough-and-tumble affair, in which science was for the moment thrown to the winds, and in which Kilrain, who came again in marvellous fashion, finished up the stronger of the pair. Time, 23 seconds.

ROUND 41—Curiously enough Smith scored heavily on the chest with both right and left, and then, ducking, cleverly avoided a terrific right-handed return. Kilrain tried again, but could not get home, and napped a very hot straight, left-handed hit, which virtually ended the round. Time, 12 seconds.

ROUND 42—Kilrain appeared fresher than for some rounds previous, but on coming to the scratch after one exchange, they closed and were struggling in holds for fully half a minute, when they fell, Smith's head being doubled under Kilrain's shoulder. Time, 36 seconds. At the end of this round some variety was imparted to the proceedings by the protestations of friendship and the handshakings of the seconds, Jack Baldock and Ned Donnelly.

ROUND 43—Smith got the worst of the fall. Time, 14 seconds.

ROUNDS 45 to 58—In all these rounds Kilrain had much the best of it.

ROUND 59—Smith at once took a commanding lead, and for 20 seconds went for Jake hammer and tongs. This was the shortest round of the fight. Kilrain eventually knocking Smith down with a swinging right-hander.

ROUND 60—Smith came up to the mark wonderfully well at first, but was a bit dazed, and after getting a couple of hot uns in the ribs, went down.

ROUND 61—Kilrain had now taken so strong a lead that he looked to have the battle won.

ROUND 62—A claim of going down without a blow was properly refused, because Smith delivered a good one, and then fell from the effects of a heavy right-hander. Time, 15 seconds.

ROUND 63—In this round Smith had slightly the best of the exchanges, and Kilrain fell from weakness.

ROUND 64—The advantage was now again on the side of Kilrain, who had the best of some fierce milling, and got Smith in holds, and clinched him for a moment, but desisted and gave ground when he heard a claim of foul threatened. Time, 41 seconds.

ROUND 65—Smith now perked up wonderfully, and thrice got on Kilrain's damaged eye, but the American retaliated with a stinging right-hander on the jaw, which staggered Smith, but recovering himself, he threw Kilrain with a back heel, and walked to his corner. Time, 30 seconds.

ROUND 66—This was a very evenly contested round, each in turn taking a lead, and a merry set-to ended by Smith popping the right on Kilrain's damaged optic. Time, 57 seconds.

ROUND 67—Smith pegged away merrily, and after receiving a heavy smack on the eye, forced Kilrain on the ropes, though they both fell. Time, 29 seconds. [At this time one or two of the natives put in an appearance, but, singularly enough, did not take any interest in the proceedings. They stood by the ring a few minutes, but then tired and chatted with the captain of the steamer.]

ROUND 68—Jem came up with a laugh to his seconds as they told him to go in and win, but Kilrain had the best of the round. Time, 24 seconds.

ROUND 69—Smith slapped a left on the ribs, and closing, had put in three warmish half-arm jobs on the ribs before Kilrain, following his usual tactics, held his opponent's disengaged hand. In the fall the Yankee dropped heavily on his man. Kilrain looked very serious as he sat in his corner. Time, 18 seconds.

ROUND 70—Not a blow was struck before the two got in hold, and nearly all the eighteen seconds the round occupied went in struggling for the fall. Smith was mending, but Kilrain was in possession of a good lead.

ROUND 71—In the hope of finishing our man off, Kilrain continued to start at him as soon as they got within distance. Smith never once flinched nor tried to spar for time. So far as he had a fair opening he always tried to hit, and Kilrain cannot complain that he was not given every opportunity for winning if he could. Time, 23 seconds.

ROUND 72—Smith was back-heeled and fell, with Kilrain on him. Time, 14 seconds.

ROUND 73—Smith began with the left on the jaw and stopped a big drive at the point, but copped the right on the mark. Kilrain scored next with his left on the mouth and a half-arm dig in the ribs, for which Jem made up with a fine left on the point. Time, 13 seconds.

ROUND 74—Kilrain looked the picture of coolness and firmness as regards his left side, on which the eye was all right. The other was all but gone, though a little bit of glimmer could be seen through it. Smith never once in the fight lost his good natured look and, as usual, was smiling as he stood up once more. Kilrain had a big lead in this round. Time, 10 seconds.

ROUND 75—Notwithstanding the heavy punishment in the round before, Smith came up promptly at time, and faced his opponent resolutely enough. Kilrain found his way with the right to the side of the jaw. Smith countered with the left on the right eye, which was beginning to puff, like its fellow. Our champion stood up as usual for some fast exchanges, but was forced down in the pully hauly business which ended the next round. Time, 23 seconds.

ROUND 76 Smith was ready for a go as they neared, and scored handsomely with the right on the ribs. He was beaten in the throw. Time, 26 seconds.

ROUND 77—In the previous round Kilrain seemed so much the stronger that Smith's friends began to fear that the turn in the tide would not come, but their pet pulled up wonderfully for the next round, and had none the worse of some fast two-handed fighting. Toward the end, after each had got a fine left in on the jaw, they fought at great pace with both hands. Jem was quite as good as the other at this game, and, what is more, was the stronger in the wrestle, and had Jake under. Time, 18 seconds.

ROUND 78—Smith again showed improvement. Very little was done before they clinched and rolled down side by side. Time, 18 seconds.

ROUND 79—Smith set to work to make the pace, and both went down. Time, 32 seconds.

ROUND 80—Kilrain opened with a damaging left-hander straight on the point, for which Jem showed himself most eager to pay. He tried twice for the face, but was short. With a fall the round closed. Time, 33 seconds.

ROUND 81—Kilrain took a lead again in this. Smith had not got a blow home when he went down. Time, 9 seconds.

ROUND 82—Kilrain led at the point, but he was cleverly stopped. He waited for Smith, who tried hard to draw him with the left. As Smith came forward he landed a terribly hot right-hander on the jaw, closed and threw the Britisher, who was in a very awkward position, with his head doubled up on his chest, and the Yankee's weight on him. Kilrain was again scoring the faster, and Smith's chance once more seemed ebbing. The few Americans were very confident, and some of the other side looked on a draw as their only chance. Time, 29 seconds.

ROUND 83—Smith opened the ball with the left at the mark, and was met with the left straight on the nose. Heavy exchanges followed till they closed, and Smith was heavily shaken as they fell. Kilrain was adding to his lead. Time, 32 seconds.

ROUND 84—The American's wind was very good, and he advanced very confidently for another try to win. He gave no rest nor quarter, and started with a smashing left on the cheek bone, to which Smith replied with a short-length on the lower ribs, which made Jake wince a bit. Smith was under in the fall. Time, 24 seconds.

ROUND 85—The cold was cruel at this period, and it was wonderful that neither of the men shivered. Smith had had a drop of brandy and it did him good. He led, and got home on the right eye. After one exchange they fell. Time, 14 seconds.

ROUND 86—Kilrain's left was on Smith's jaw after the first attempt, and the counter stopped. In the fall Kilrain came with all his weight on to the other. Time, 23 seconds.

ROUND 87—Kilrain reached the nose with the left and followed, while Jem was a little bit turned, with a fearful smash on the left ear which sent Smith down, and ought to have settled the fight had our man not been so tough. The third right-hand knock-down made matters very serious for the Englishmen's hopes. Time, 17 seconds.

ROUND 68—Jem, always game, came up promptly, and, to the general astonishment, opened with a pretty left-hander on the mark. He was at once driven back with the right on the chest and got down. Time, 5 seconds.

ROUND 89—Smith's start was with the left at the ribs, a blow which landed, but drew a smart punch on the point. Just as the pair were standing up to hit fast, Smith slipped and fell with his head against a stake. Time, 7 seconds.

JOHN FLEMING.   GEORGE W. ATKINSON.

ROUND 90—After a spar for a few seconds they closed, and in a hard go for the fall, Jem fairly twisted the other over. Time, 12 seconds.

ROUND 91—Jem's pluck was wonderful, but so was Kilrain's, for though he the advantage, he had been heavily punished. Jem scored with his left on the throat. Kilrain got in a curious sort of uppercut on the ribs with his right. The round ended in 16 seconds with a dog fall.

ROUND 92—Smith's chance was looking up again in the previous round or two, and improved again in this. Kilrain was the first with the left on the ribs. He followed with a grand right on the jaw, which seemed as though it must knock anyone out. To the wonder of all who saw the blow, Smith stood his ground, countered on the point with his left, and in the wrestle put Kilrain down, while he himself kept his feet. Time, 15 seconds.

ROUND 93—No blow struck. Smith under in the fall. Time, 11 seconds.

ROUND 94—After a jangle between the seconds, Smith just missed getting in a big right-hander on the good eye. Per contra he just dodged a warm right-hander from the Yank. Jem got the left on the neck twice in succession, slipped under a vicious right at the head, and got down. Time, 15 seconds.

ROUND 95—At this time the light was growing dim, and as Smith was very strong on his legs, in fact, getting stronger instead of weaker, there seemed prospects of a draw for the day without a settlement. After two or three exchanges the round came to a scrambling finish. Time, 16 seconds.

ROUND 96—After a counter in which little harm was done, Kilrain got Smith round the neck with his left, and put in a couple of hot rib binders with his right, Smith going under in the fall. Time, 14 seconds.

ROUND 97—This did look as though it must settle Jem. Kilrain was all over him. The American dashed him in the eye twice with his left, got at the left ear with the right, a very hard drive; then as our man staggered sent in the left on the chin and the right on the neck. Smith fell backward from the effects of these last two blows. Time, 11 seconds.

ROUND 98—Mitchell and Co. reasonably looked on the fight as won. Kilrain was bent on making sure of the win there and then. Smith met him with a straight left on the right eye, but got a fearful ram in the left ribs from the other's right. As they closed and fell Smith dropped away from the Yank, who actually stopped his weight from coming on his prostrate foe by putting out his hands—a fine piece of character work. Time, 38 seconds.

ROUND 99—Smith stopped three or four hot ones, and kept his man at a distance till at last the Yank's right landed once more on the left ear. They fell together. Time, 15 seconds.

ROUND 100—Kilrain led, and landed with the left low in the body. Smith tripped in stepping back from the next lead, and Kilrain, who fell over him, got up and walked by himself to his corner. Time, 16 seconds.

ROUND 102—Smith's show after the 101st round was almost miraculous. He opened with a pretty left on the chin and stopped the counter. Next he scored with a pile driver on the point from the left, one of, if not the heaviest blow he had got in. Before the scramble Smith had another good left on the ribs, and was stronger of the two in the fall. Time, 17 seconds.

ROUND 103—Before a straight blow had been struck they were wrestling, in which Smith had the best. Time, 8 seconds.

ROUND 104—The light was going so fast that it was quite difficult to see the watch hands. Smith set to work as if he had made up his mind to finish Kilrain, as Kilrain had failed to finish him while he was weak. He got about as briskly as if he had not doneany work or been hit. Jem opened with the left on the right eye, which was just about closed. Kilrain replied with the left and right on neck and cheek. Then they sparred for a moment. Kilrain led at the point, was stopped; tried at the face, and was short. Smith, also failed to get far enough. Just before the end of the round, which lasted 36 seconds, Smith put in a useful drive on the ear with the left, which was paid for with a good right-hander on the left ear. They fell together at the finish of a very even round.

[An appeal had before this been raised to suspend hostilities, because of the bad light, but not complied with].

ROUND 105—Smith led with the left at the mouth, but was countered on the chest. After three or four exchanges Kilrain got a good right on the ear, but matters were equalized with a left and right on neck and chin. Smith beat his man in the wrestle. Time, 23 seconds.

ROUND 106 AND LAST—The appeal for adjourning was again raised. Mr. Atkinson decided to have one more round, and then leave off. Both worked fast in this. Smith scored with his left on the mouth, and had to take a good right in the ribs. They had three or four fast exchanges in the middle of the ring, and in the end fell together. As the round ended there was nothing to choose between the men. Perhaps Smith was the stronger. Kilrain had got rather weaker in the last few rounds, while Smith had pulled himself together. At the announcement of an adjournment the two game fellows stood in the middle of the ring and both smiled pleasantly as they cordially shook hands. Then all made for the steamers, to hear what would be done about the renewal of hostilities.

WM. E. HARDING AND CHARLEY MITCHELL TALK.

To the Editor of Sporting Life :

SIR—At the time Mr. Richard K. Fox, the recognized King of Sportsmen in the New World, met Jem Smith, the champion of England, and his able manager, Mr. John Fleming, at the *Sporting Life* office on July 26 last, to arrange the great international prize fight between America's genuine champion, Jake Kilrain, and Jem Smith, the recognized champion of England, for the "Police Gazette" diamond belt, $10,000 and the championship of the world, knowing prophets stated that the battle would never take place, and if the men ever met in the ring that English sporting men would not give Kilrain fair play.

Again, when it was known that Charley Mitchell had decided to act as Kilrain's mentor, and officiate as his *fidus Achates*, they assailed Mitchell and even went so far as to say that Kilrain would not be fairly dealt with, and that Mitchell would prove a second Judas Iscariot. This influenced a certain section of the American sporting public actually to believe that the American champion would not receive fair play. Nevertheless, Mr. Richard K. Fox, the leading promoter of all legitimate and manly sporting pastimes, had full confidence in Charley Mitchell and the many followers of the P. R. in England, and, in spite of the earnest solicitations of Americans not to allow Kilrain to remain under the mentorship of Charley Mitchell, decided not only to go ahead with the match, but agreed that Mitchell should second and train the American champion. On behalf of Mr. Richard K. Fox, whom I represent, I desire through the *Sporting Life*, the leading sporting newspaper in England, to thank the English public for the kind treatment and fair play Kilrain (our American champion) has received during his stay in this country. It will be emblazoned in history that with but three Americans outside the ring, Kilrain made a desperate and protracted struggle with his courageous opponent, which will be recorded in fistic chronology as one of the greatest encounters ever fought in modern times. I have witnessed Aaron Jones fight Mike McCoole, and every battle fought in the land of Stars and Stripes since that time. The two best and most determined battles I ever witnessed were Jem Mace's battle with Tom Allen for $5,000 and the championship of the world, at New Orleans, May 10, 1870, and the great international battle between Jem Smith, England's pending champion, and Jake Kilrain, the champion of America, on the island in the Seine, France, on December 19. No matter what any one may say or write about the last great international battle, Smith proved himself one of the gamest men I ever saw in face of an opponent in fistic array, and well worthy, too, to sustain the title of English champion, which he holds, whilst Kilrain's fistic abilities exceeded my anticipations, as he proved himself superior to any pugilist who ever fought for the championship of America. Not wishing to encroach too much on your valuable space, I desire to thank Charley Mitchell for the able manner in which he piloted and esquired the American champion, also Ned Donnelly, Charley Rowell, Mr. George W. Moore and Mr. Geo. W. Atkinson, of the *Sporting Life*, who acted as referee, and discharged his duties honorably and fairly to all concerned. To Mr. J. Fleming, who made the excellent arrangements for bringing off the fight, which were carried out in the most praiseworthy manner, my thanks are also due.
Yours, &c.,   WILLIAM E. HARDING,
                              Representative of Richard K. Fox, backer of Kilrain.

To the Editor of Sporting Life :

SIR—Sullivan, the bogus champion, is at his old game again, and seeks to make capital out of the recent international fight by challenging both men at a time when he should have held his peace. When he is through with me I don't think he will want any more engagements under New Prize Ring Rules, for I am vain enough to fancy he will then realize the fact that he is not a "fistic marvel." Sullivan has only fought once, and then with a man who did not rank higher than a selling plater. Having refused to

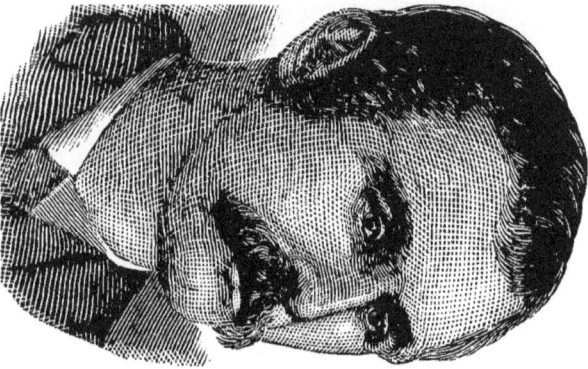

CHARLEY HOWELL.

PROF. NED DONNELLY.

light Kilrain before he left America, I am sure nobody will believe Sullivan is in earnest now. If so, let him cover Mr. Richard K. Fox's deposit of $200. Following so closely on the recent gallant fight, Sullivan's challenge is unworthy of notice, and if he takes my tip he will let the matter rest, as I. consider it is a monkey to a pony on Kilrain or Jem Smith whipping him. Yours, etc.,   CHARLES MITCHELL,
                                                        English Boxing Champion.

PRESS OPINIONS ON THE FIGHT.

THE SMITH-KILRAIN FIGHT—A CARD FROM THE SUN REPORTER WHO SAW IT FROM

BEGINNING TO END.

TO THE EDITOR OF THE SUN—*Sir:* A word about the Smith-Kilrain fight.
I saw it from start to finish, knew the men personally, saw them before the fight at Rouen, and afterward for two days in Paris and London. As the mill went on I made a record of every one of the 106 rounds, and I write now, after a review of this history in conjunction with other information picked up at first hand. As the press is still burdened by the authoritative and haughty opinions of men who did not see the fight, a word from an actual witness may be of value.
The assertion that the fight was a "barney," or not sincere, is nonsense, pure, bald and silly. Smith was not knocked out for the following reasons:
FIRST—He was young, strong, perfectly trained, plucky, and almost as good a man as Kilrain.
SECOND—The ground was marshy, "sopping wet," and covered by a thick growth of grass at least ten inches long. It became so well matted by the feet of the pugilists after the sixth round that it was as soft as a Jersey feather bed when Smith fell on it, and he was clever enough to keel over rapidly whenever the work got too hot for him.
THIRD—The half minute rest between rounds under the new prize ring rules gave Smith considerably more than an hour's rest during the mill. He needed it throughout. Kilrain did not.
FOURTH—The referee showed a leaning toward his countryman. It was not dark when the fight was called. At that time Smith was weak, staggering, and so evidently beaten that his supporters had nearly all walked indifferently away from the ring, feeling that the defeat of their man was inevitable. Kilrain was firm and confident. He and Mitchell both begged for a continuance of the fight, if only for three rounds. Smith had had enough.
The Englishman fought recklessly and took every chance, because he knew that every fluke and foul would be turned to his credit by his countrymen, including the referee. On the other hand, Kilrain lost many an opportunity that might have won the fight, because he knew that the slightest irregularity on his part would be instantly turned against him.
Charles Mitchell was as staunch, true and honest a second on this occasion as ever followed a fighter into a ring. W. E. Harding did not show any unfriendliness to Kilrain.
I know nothing about the charges of conspiracy, etc., which are so prominent in the papers just now. I have small respect for the pugilists, plug uglies, and schemers who make their living out of the ring to-day, but as far as the fight itself was concerned, it was unquestionably straight up and up. Both tried to win—Kilrain on his merits, Smith by hook or crook and the favor of his friends.
                                                        BLAKELEY HALL.
HOTEL SHELBOURNE, DUBLIN, Feb. 12.

The time has come for those who may still be disposed to cry "fake," in the face of this overwhelming proof to the contrary, to bring forward something stronger and more convincing than idle assertions, backed up with slander and vituperation. Talk is cheap. What the public and the sporting fraternity want are facts. But as the "fake" champions have done nothing but talk, we do not expect that they will remain silent so long as there are a few fools left who will believe their silly charges.—POLICE GAZETTE.
The New York *Clipper*, of world-wide fame as an authority on pugilism, says this:
The parties interested in the management of the match between Jake Kilrain, the American champion, and Jem Smith champion of England, for the championship of the world, $5,000 a side and the belt offered by Richard K. Fox of this city, backer of Kilrain, anticipated the original fixture, Jan. 3 next, and brought off the battle on Monday last,

and on French soil, instead of in Spain. This precaution was taken in order to lessen the probability of interference by the authorities or otherwise, and it attested the earnest desire on the part of all concerned to have the question between the rival champions settled by an appeal to the code, thereby proving how wrong were those on both sides of the Atlantic who, ever since the agreement was entered into, have persisted in asserting that business was at no time intended, and that the principals would never be found in a ring together.

The character of the battle itself certainly proved that the combatants themselves were very much in earnest. It was one of the most protracted pugilistic battles ever contested within the ropes, and for such heavy men to stand before each other for two hours and a half, during the greater part of which time they were engaged in some of the fastest fighting ever witnessed, even among light-weights, was astonishing, and shows that both are blessed with unusual powers of endurance, and that each was trained to the hour for the engagement. Although it was admitted that the American was the more skillful boxer, besides possessing an undoubted advantage in the matter of length of reach, the general impression among those who would seem best qualified to form a correct judgment in regard to the subject was that the sturdy Englishman would at least oustay his antagonist, even if he did not, as they confidently anticipated, prove the better punisher and the fiercer, more bull-dog-like fighter.

To size it all up, they did not think that there was enough of the "devil" in the American's composition to properly back up his skill and undoubted gameness when opposed by such a thorough, persevering pugilist as the British champion. All through the battle, however, Kilrain was the aggressor, and at all points he outfought and outgeneraled his adversary, notwithstanding the fact the latter proved himself as good as anticipated, except in the matter of wrestling, wherein he had been expected to greatly excel, whereas he gained nothing from his knowledge of the science. The performance of the American stamps him as a better man by considerable than the majority, even of his own countrymen, gave him credit for being, and it is safe to say that he will meet with a hearty welcome when he returns to our shores. He had unquestionably the better of the contest from end to end, and had there been light enough to finish it on the day he would no doubt have won, provided he had received fair play to the last. It is unfortunate that the battle was not renewed, and no doubt that there are many who will blame Kilrain for agreeing to a draw, especially when his superiority had been so clearly established. It is probable, however, that he had reason to believe that had they met again the battle would not have been decided on the merits of the men, as considerable money depended on the issue, and it was not unreasonable to fear that the opposite side, who were largely in the ascendency, would resort to unfair means to save the same, now that the inability of their representative to win by fair fighting had been made apparent to all at the ring-side. If he did not succeed in capturing the laurels outright, Jake has at least the satisfaction of knowing that he clearly demonstrated his ability to have done so had the opportunity been afforded him. It is not probable that these men will ever meet again and we presume that the previously broached match between Kilrain and John L. Sullivan will be made, as the backer of the former is now more willing than ever to find the necessary amount to match the champion against the Boston Boy in a fight with the bare knuckles.

Evening Post.—At this festive season of the year it is usual in sporting, as in other circles, to slow down a bit, but on the present occasion the section of the community that concerns itself with racing and kindred sports seems to be steaming along at high pressure. The boom is just now boxing and prize fighting, and it seems we have caught on with the general public almost as much as with the sporting community. For some time past exhibitions with the gloves have been on the increase, and occasionally a contest with those weapons has been fought *a outrance* until one of the combatants has failed to respond to the cry of "Time!" From boxing under Queensberry rules to fighting with the 'raw 'uns" is an easy step, and it is only natural that patrons of lads after witnessing their prowess with the gloves should desire to see how they shape with them off. The little sporting coterie known as the Pelican Club is responsible for much of the present rise in fisticuffs. Week after week the proprietor has organized exhibitions of the manly art, and the keenness with which every round was watched by the spectators showed clearly the way the wind was blowing. The late fight between Smith and Kilrain is the precursor of many another battle, and so long as the roughs of the ring who did so much to bring prize fighting into disrepute a couple of decades ago are kept off, there is no reason why it should not form a staple amusement for the young bloods who are growing weary of the somewhat epicene amusements of the metropolis.

The Latrobe (Pa.) Advance.—America has now, not only the champion pugilist of the world in Jake Kilrain, but the champion "backer" also in Richard K. Fox, whose liberality in presenting his man with the entire stakes has never been equalled. Now

THE "POLICE GAZETTE" DIAMOND BELT,

THE RECOGNIZED EMBLEM OF THE HEAVY-WEIGHT CHAMPIONSHIP OF THE WORLD.

for Sullivan : Mr. Fox has the money and Kilrain the muscle which say the ex-champion is the *ex*-champion and all that is necessary is for Jno. L. to toe the mark and fight instead of junketing around with the snobs of England. If we were to begin giving Sullivan lessons in truthfulness we'd have him write Richard K. Fox as follows : "I must beg to acknowledge that I am unable to meet Kilrain because I am convinced that he is superior to me as a fighter. My many battles with John Barleycorn have fitted me for nothing except a side show attraction."

New York Sun.—Mr. Richard K. Fox, the boss patron of the prize ring in this country, says he will never rest until he finds some man who can knock out the Hon. John Lawrence Sullivan. He does not care how long it will take or what it will cost; he will not rest until he finds a man who can down the only champion. Mr. Fox has undertaken a very big job. The peerless John is very anxious to meet any man with sufficient reputation to command his august consideration, and the world will applaud Mr. Fox if he can produce as much muscle and science as are represented in the Boston phenomenon.

A BOSTON WOMAN WHO ADMIRES KILRAIN.

Boston Post.—The recent reports of the terrible fight between Kilrain and Smith emphasize several facts. First, that the love for gladiatorial contests for which old Rome was so remarkable is not dead, but rising constantly into more vigorous life among us through the efforts of the sporting editors of our daily papers; second, that English gentlemen of noble lineage are not ashamed to be known as lawbreakers in the matter of sustaining the prize ring; and, lastly, the English pugilistic champion, Smith, is a brutal slugger and not a legitimate exponent of the art of boxing. Just here I desire to express the wish that when Smith and Sullivan meet to settle the championship they will exterminate each other as effectively as the Kilkenny cats; though this is too much to hope.

Now, what I wish to observe with regard to Kilrain, who is said to be a Connecticut blacksmith of Irish extraction, is this : Viewing the matter apart from the consideration of its brutality and illegality, we have got to admit two things; first, to be a pugilist at all obliges a man to be first a hard worker, and next abstemious in regard to all sensual indulgences or excesses, which are two fundamental qualities in the make-up of what we call a man. But Kilrain has shown something more than immense pluck and muscle. He has shown character. The manner in which he was dressed, the small number of his friends (I believe they were but three), his modest demeanor, and his splendid temper, show the man to be something far above the average bruiser. Indeed, he intimated so much that was fine in this fight that he ought never to fight again, unless providence has expressly sent him to "knock out" John Sullivan. I would suggest to the athletic clubs of this country, therefore, that they invite Kilrain to return home and give him a gymnasium of his own, where he can train the rising generation in athletics and also in this fine art of keeping one's temper. In this way Kilrain would never have to soil his fingers with another bully of any nationality. His behavior in that fight seems to show that he has undeveloped capacity for being a gentleman. A hero, though, alas! a perverted hero, he now is. Let his countrymen give him a chance to be something better.

I trust some friend of his may send him a copy of these lines.

A MOTHER OF SONS.

WM. E. HARDING: "There never was a prize fight so well contested by two heavyweight champions. Kilrain is the hardest hitter, the best wrestler and the coolest and most determined pugilist I have seen since Jem Mace faced Tom Allen at Kenner Station, Louisiana, on May 10, 1870. Kilrain possesses all the necessary points so essential to be a champion beyond a doubt, for he entered a twenty-four foot ring on foreign soil, with only a few friends, not knowing whether he would receive fair play or foul. It was his initial battle in the prize ring according to London prize ring rules. Few except his backer, Richard K. Fox; Charley Mitchell, his manager, and myself, the representative of Richard K. Fox, had any idea that Kilrain could fight according to prize ring rules. Many claimed he could not wrestle, that he only had one hand to box with, that Sullivan was his peer, etc. Notwithstanding all the enemies Kilrain had to contend against, he faced the English champion for two hours and thirty-one minutes, winning first blood, first knock-down, and would, without any doubt, have defeated Smith had the daylight lasted twenty minutes longer. He was strong at the finish and ready to continue the struggle."

To be handed to
"Jake Kilrain"
when he enters the Sing to
bet on himself.

Richard K. Fox.

THE ENDORSEMENT ON THE BACK.

a terrific blow in the mouth, and for a time he deemed it prudent to resort to what is known as the "getting down" tactics, with a view to snatching as much rest as possible. During the last twenty rounds a teaspoonful of brandy was administered to the Londoner after each bout, but it was noticeable from beginning to end of the fight Kilrain never took any stimulant whatever. All that his seconds did was to occasionally wipe his tongue with a sponge.

Sporting Chronicle.—Those who had pooh-poohed the idea of any fight resulting from the visit of the American pugilist to this country, as well as another section of know-alls, who scouted the idea of Jake Kilrain being able to stand up for any length of time before our champion, Jem Smith, must feel wonderfully small just at present. The fight has taken place, and that, too, without those objectionable surroundings which have done so much to bring the noble art into disrepute. There has not been the suspicion of a barney about the whole affair, while last but by no means least, the "blatent Yankee," the "mean pretender," the "hippodromist," as Jake Kilrain has frequently been termed, has stood like a man for 106 hard-fought rounds and, taking the proceedings all through, did not have, by any means, the worst of the battle. Those who fancied that Kilrain did not show his real form when sparring Mitchell were not mistaken, and we could point out almost innumerable instances in which men who gained high places on the muster roll of past champions have been failures with the gloves. Take Tom Sayers as an example. It is doubtful if England ever produced a better man at his weight, but when muzzled he was a comparative fraud.

Evening News, Belfast, Ireland.—One has to hark back to the year 1860 ere finding a record of an important international fight for the championship. It was on the 17th of April in that year that the never-to-be-forgotten meeting between Tom Sayers and John C. Heenan took place at Farnborough. Every lover of the sport can tell how, after 2 hours and 6 minutes hot work, the ring was invaded by the crowd, and eventually the fight was declared a draw. Matters went from bad to worse with the institution until Mr. R. K. Fox, an American sporting journalist, well-known in Belfast, who had taken the new fistic star, Kilrain, in hand, visited this country, and after rather less "paper warfare" than is customary in such matters, met Jem Smith and his supporters in London, July 26th, 1887, and made the match that we have already stated was the first important international fight for a period of 27 years.

Manchester Examiner.—The revival of interest in the prize ring has been of gradual but steady growth. Though the fights are illegal the publication of the reports of them, filled with the most sickening details and described in the most atrocious slang, are not an offence against our criminal code. An Irish Nationalist journal, whose editor would be liable to a month's imprisonment if he printed the most innocuous paragraph about a league meeting in a proclaimed district might fill its pages with elaborate and stimulating accounts of a fight in which two men mauled each other's face to a pulp or gouged out each other's eyes. It is pitiable to find that some London daily journals boasting of a great circulation do not hesitate to pander to a low taste by publishing this morning, no doubt at a great cost for reporting and telegraphing, the fullest and most odious particulars of the fight which took place yesterday on an obscure island in the Seine.

Fred Gallagher, editor of *Sport*, Dublin, Ireland, an eye witness of the big fight, says: "In the whole history of the prize ring no fight has been conducted under better auspices, honored as it was with the patronage of a most aristocratic company. Kilrain kept his head from start to finish. He is clever, and with the raw'uns a fine natural hitter. There is no mistaking his fighting abilities. A quieter, cooler, more dogged fellow than Jake Kilrain never lived."

A CHAT WITH JEM MACE.

The correspondent visited Jem Mace, who is now an instructor of boxing at Wair's School of Arms near Regent street quadrant. He bears his fifty years remarkably well, and looked as if he could come up smiling and fresh for many rounds. Mace had read all the details of the fight. He thought that while Smith had not been properly extended in his French contest with Greenfield, yesterday Smith seemed to have been fully extended by Kilrain. Mace said that the American was better than he had thought him. He considered the fight a tough one, reflecting credit on both. He drew a distinction between a boxer and a fighter, and added: "I am now a boxer and not a fighter. The man with the hardest knuckles and the greatest endurance will invariably win, even over the best boxer lacking in these points."

ORIGIN OF THE GREAT INTERNATIONAL PRIZE FIGHT

BETWEEN JAKE KILRAIN OF BOSTON, CHAMPION OF AMERICA, AND JEM SMITH, OF LON-

DON, CHAMPION OF ENGLAND.

The great International prize fight for the "Police Gazette" diamond belt, $10,000 and the championship of the world between Jake Kilrain, of Boston, champion of America, and Jem Smith of London, champion of England, came about in this way: Early in May, 1886, Richard K. Fox, who backed Paddy Ryan in 1882 to fight John L. Sullivan for $5,000 and the championship of America, offered to back John L. Sullivan to fight Jem Smith, the British champion, for $10,000 a side, the "Police Gazette," diamond belt, and the prize ring championship of the world. Sullivan had agreed to meet the British champion providing Mr. Fox would back him. A challenge was sent to the *Sporting Life*, London, England, and no sooner was it published than Smith at once agreed to meet the American champion. Just as the preliminaries were to be arranged the champion, to the infinite disgust of all fair-minded sporting men, backed out and allowed the British lion to roar. In the meantime Richard K. Fox, being eager to find a true champion to represent America in an international contest with the English champion, after looking up all the heavy-weights, found Jake Kilrain, a sturdy, muscular boxer who had figured in numerous contests. He held a long interview with Kilrain and found that he was ready to fight any man in the world. Richard K. Fox at once decided to match him to fight Sullivan, and agreed, if he succeeded in winning the championship, that he would match him to fight Jem Smith, the English champion.

On May 30, 1887, Richard K. Fox sent $1,000 forfeit to the New York *Clipper* with the following sweeping challenge:

NEW YORK, May 20, 1887.

Editor New York Clipper:

It being the universal desire of the sporting public to witness a battle in the arena between John L. Sullivan, the champion pugilist of America, and Jake Kilrain, the new aspirant for the title, my representative, Mr. Wm. E. Harding, with my full instructions, has done all that is possible to bring about a meeting between Mr. Sullivan and Mr. Kilrain. It is always customary for a champion, if he be a champion, to defend that title against all comers and accept all challenges. The fair and manly defi issued by myself on behalf of Jake Kilrain has not yet been replied to, although $1,000 was posted at your office to prove that the offer was *bona fide*. Now to prove to the public that Mr. Kilrain can be matched against Mr. Sullivan for $5,000 a side, articles of agreement are enclosed which are almost a *fac simile* of the agreement that Paddy Ryan and John L. Sullivan signed in 1881, in the only match Mr. Sullivan ever engaged in for the championship. The battle can be fought, if Mr. Sullivan so desires, either in Mexico or Australia, to which latter country I understand Mr. Sheedy has undertaken to convey him. If the terms suit, my representative will meet Mr. Sheedy any time he names to sign them. If Mr. Sullivan refuses, then Mr. Kilrain will claim the championship, and in my opinion be justly entitled it.

Yours truly,

RICHARD K. FOX.

No attention was paid to the first gun, and two weeks after the above defi had been issued Kilrain's backer sent the following to the New York *Clipper* :

Knowing that Kilrain has never been defeated, that he never shirked meeting a foe in manly combat, no matter whether he was a native or a foreigner, I have decided to espouse the cause of the Baltimorean, and desire through the medium of your well-known journal, the *Clipper*. to state that I will match Mr. Kilrain to meet Mr. Sullivan with gloves according to the London rules for five thousand ($5,000) dollars a side and upwards and the "Police Gazette" diamond belt, which represents the heavy-weight championship of the world, the contest to take place within a reasonable distance from Baltimore or Pittsburg, a limited number of spectators to be present, six months from signing articles, or sooner or later, at the option of Mr. Sullivan ; the New York *Clipper* to be temporary stakeholder, if acceptable, and the other details to be arranged at the time of signing articles. In order to prove to all concerned that Kilrain is in earnest to meet the champion, I enclose a certified check for one thousand ($1,000) dollars for

The Sporting Life

Kilrain v Smith

28th Dec. 1887

RECEIVED of the Proprietor of THE SPORTING LIFE
the sum of One Thousand pounds ———— shillings ————
being the amount of Stakes deposited ———— by Mr R & K. Fox
for my match with Jem Smith, for the Championship
of the World.

£1000 . 0 . 0

John L. ————
Champion of the World

JAKE KILRAIN'S RECEIPT TO THE LONDON "SPORTING LIFE" FOR ONE THOUSAND POUNDS.

the first deposit for Mr. Sullivan to cover any time this challenge is accepted. William E. Harding, my representative, will meet Mr. Sullivan or his backers at the *Clipper* office to arrange the match for as large or small a sum as a stake as Mr. Sheedy or Mr. Sullivan may desire. Should Mr. Sullivan fail within two weeks to accept Kilrain's straightforward challenge and cover the $1,000 deposited with the New York *Clipper*, Kilrain will claim the championship and receive the diamond belt. Tom Hyer had to meet Sullivan when the former was champion. The latter in turn had to meet Morrissey when Sullivan held the championship, and so it has been according to fistic chronology for the last six decades, thus establishing the law that a champion when challenged must either retire or accept. Trusting that Mr. Sullivan and his backers will toe the scratch and put up their money and arrange a match in a fair and sportsmanlike manner, I remain   RICHARD K. FOX.

Editorially, in regard to the above the *Daily News* said :

"Now that $1,000 has been posted and an official challenge issued there is no loophole for Sullivan or his manager to beat a retreat. Kilrain has a backer who will not weaken even if Sullivan's backer should talk big money. In the challenge the backer of Kilrain says six months later or sooner, so that Sheedy will have no excuse, neither will the champion, in regard to his injured arm. The stakes are fixed to the amount Sullivan proposed time and again to battle for, for $1,000 is the regular amount of stakes, and according to rule that is the amount championship matches are to be fought for, but as the champion always had a desire to contend for a large sum there is no limit, for the challenge says from '$5,000 a side and upward.' Should it be necessary, or if Sheedy should influence Sullivan to refuse to fight for $5,000, we know where $10,000 can be raised for Kilrain. Kilrain is a favorite in Baltimore, Boston and this city. Sporting men in both hemispheres will eagerly watch the moves made by the rival champions on the pugilistic checker-board, and, if Sullivan refuses to arrange a match in the face of such a bold challenge, backed up by a big forfeit, the sporting world on both sides of the Atlantic will wonder. It is well a well-known fact that all champions had to pick up the gauntlet when it had been thrown down to them. Before Sullivan ascended the pugilistic throne, Paddy Ryan was the champion, having fairly won the title by defeating Joe Goss at Collier Station, West Virginia. Ryan did not make any excuse about stakes, conditions, etc. He held the title of champion and had to defend it according to rules governing the championship. Sullivan challenged, and when Richard K. Fox, Ryan's backer, desired to make the match for $5,000, Sullivan's backer refused and would only fight for $2,500 a side. After the match was made Sullivan could not find the stakes and but for James Keenan, of Boston, Ryan would have won the money then up, for Sullivan would have forfeited. Kilrain now stands in nearly the same position in 1887 as Sullivan did in 1882, except that he has a backer who will not let the match fall through if the champion is ready to defend his title, but as far as the rules are concerned it is a well-known fact, that no championship contest can be contended for where the number of rounds fought are limited. Sullivan will have to agree to battle by London rules with small gloves. By these rules he won the title of championship and therefore will have to go the same journey to keep it, if the match is arranged, and it will be the fault of Sullivan and his backers if it is not. It will create a furore."

Sullivan did not accept the challenge and claimed that if he had not broken his arm Kilrain would never have challenged him. Richard K. Fox announced that he could name his own time to fight, six months, eight months or a year, and this liberal offer offset all Sullivan's excuses. Sullivan was allowed one month to cover the $1,900 posted at the *Clipper* office, and it was publicly announced that if Sullivan did not defend his title of champion Kilrain would claim the title and fight all comers for the "Police Gazette" diamond belt. Finding Sullivan would not fight, Kilrain offered to fight any man in America for $2,500 and upwards. As there was found to be no boxer in America who had the money or courage to meet Kilrain, he was declared champion of America, and on June 4, 1887, the "Police Gazette" diamond belt, which was offered by Richard K. Fox, to represent the heavy-weight championship of the world, was presented to Kilrain at the Monumental Theatre, Baltimore, Maryland. On receiving the championship belt, Kilrain agreed to defend it according to the rules and regulations governing the same against any man in the world.

On June 20 $1,000 was posted with the New York *Clipper*, and Richard K. Fox authorized Kilrain to issue a challenge to fight Jem Smith, of London, England, who claimed the title of champion of the world, because John L. Sullivan, when champion in 1886, refused to fight Smith after he had challenged the English champion, and the latter agreed to fight Sullivan in Ireland. One thousand dollars was posted and the following defi was published :

"Jake Kilrain, the American champion, having vainly tried to bring about an engagement with John L. Sullivan, the late champion, without success, and, although $1,000 was posted and a challenge issued for Kilrain to meet all comers, no reply was made, neither was the champion's forfeit covered, so that he has decided to meet England's champion in the roped ring for the premier position in pugilism, the championship, and as large a sum as Smith's (the English champion) backers desire to put up. Advices from England state that Smith's backers are ready to back him to fight any man breathing according to the orthodox rules, in a 24-foot ring for from £100 to £500 a side and the championship of the world, and to prove whether they are in earnest to-day one thousand dollars was posted at the *Clipper* office, and the following challenge forwarded to the *Sporting Life*, London, Eng., for the English champion to accept or refuse to do so."

The champion of America's greeting to the champion of England:

"NEW YORK, June, 1887.

"Editor Sporting Life, Strand, London, England.

"In order to gratify admirers of athletic sports who desire to witness fair and manly struggles for the supremacy between men aspiring to the title of champion of the prize ring, and in reply to the recent bold defi issued by Jem Smith, the champion pugilist of the English prize ring, to meet any man in the world face to face within the orthodox 24-foot ring for the championship of the world and $5,000 a side, I make the following fair proposition: I will meet Jem Smith according to the new rules of the London prize ring for the sum of $2,500 or $5,000 a side, the championship of the world and the "Police Gazette" diamond belt, with small gloves, or if his backer objects, without them. The contest to be decided six months from signing articles of agreement. In regard to the battle ground I prefer United States soil, and will allow Smith the sum of $500 for expenses. If Smith is satisfied with this agreement, which is forwarded by my backer, Mr. Richard K. Fox, of New York, it can be signed and returned to me for my signature. To prove I am in earnest, Mr. Fox has deposited $1,000 (£200) forfeit with the New York *Clipper* in this city.

"John C. Heenan and Tom Sayers fought in 1860 on English soil and did not succeed in bringing the battle to a termination. Therefore I think I am justified in selecting either the United States, Ireland, Spain or France for the battle ground. I am ready to defend the "Police Gazette" diamond belt against all comers, and all I ask is no favors but fair field, and may the best man win. Trusting the match will be promptly and satisfactorily arranged, I remain.

"JAKE KILRAIN,
"Champion of America."

After Kilrain's challenge was issued and $1,000 put up to back it, Jem Smith, the British champion, accepted the defi and agreed to fight Kilrain, at the same time putting up a deposit with George W. Atkinson at the *Sporting Life*, London, England. After Richard K. Fox, Kilrain's backer, ascertained that the English champion had decided to meet Kilrain, he decided to go over to England and in person arrange the preliminaries for the historical match. On July 2, 1887, Richard K. Fox sailed for England on board the Cunard steamer "Etruria," bringing with him a draft for $20,000, which he had decided to put up on the American champion providing the British champion's backers were willing to arrange the match for that sum.

On it being announced in the English sporting press that the American champion's backer had arrived in England there was a great sensation in sporting circles. A day was agreed upon for the meeting of Smith and his backers at the *Sporting Life* office and promptly at the time named for the important meeting a tremendous crowd was present.

Promptly at the time named, Richard K. Fox was on hand ready to ratify the match. Mr. George Atkinson of the *Sporting Life*, proceeded to read the articles of agreement, the following gentlemen being present: Mr. Jem Smith, champion of England, Mr. J. Fleming, the champion's manager, Mr. R. K. Fox, proprietor of the New York *Police Gazette*, Mr. E. A. Perry, correspondent of the Boston *Herald*, Mr. Bonsall, New York *World*, Mr. T. J. Bulling, Cable News Company, New York, Mr. Arthur Brisbane, New York *Sun*, Mr. James Nixon, *Melbourne Sportsman*, Mr. Bob Habbijam, Mr. Jack Harper and Major Burke, the well-known *attache* of the Wild Westeries. We append the articles of agreement:

ARTICLES OF AGREEMENT entered into this day (Tuesday, July 26, 1887), between Jake Kilrain of Baltimore, Maryland, U. S. A., and James Smith of London, England. The said Jake Kilrain and James Smith hereby agree to fight a fair stand up fight according to the new rules of the London prize ring, by which the said Jake Kilrain and the said James Smith hereby mutually agree to be bound. The said fight shall be for £1,000 ($5,000) a side and the *Police Gazette* diamond belt (now held by Jake Kilrain), value $2,500, which represents the championship of the world, and shall take place on

JAKE ALWAYS ON TOP.

CROSS BUTTOCK.

CLOSE FIGHTING.

THE ENGLISHMAN GETS DOWNED AGAIN.

KILRAIN'S UNDER-CUT.

IN SMITH'S CORNER.

Monday, Jan. 3, 1888, or on any other day within six months from signing these articles. The fight to take place within 100 miles of Madrid, Spain. Each man (Smith and Kilrain) to have a representative to act on his behalf, Mr. Richard K. Fox to appoint the representative to act for Kilrain. The two representatives to select the battle ground, issue all invitations (not exceeding 50 persons a side), and carry out the arrangements for bringing off the fight. In pursuance of this agreement £200 ($1,000) has been deposited in the hands of the New York *Clipper* by Mr. Richard K. Fox, N. Y. (proprietor of the *Police Gazette*), the backer of Jake Kilrain; and the said Jem Smith this day (Tuesday, July 26), deposits £200 with the editor of the *Sporting Life*, to be forwarded by the last-named to the New York *Clipper* to cover Kilrain's deposit, and to bind the match. The remaining deposits to be staked at the *Sporting Life* office as follows: £200 a side on Friday, Aug. 26, 1887: £200 a side on Friday, September 23, 1887: £200 a side on Friday, October 21, 1887: and the final deposit of £200 a side on Friday, November 25, 1887, when Smith must also stake with the *Sporting Life* £100, to be handed over to Mr. Richard K. Fox on behalf of Jake Kilrain as expenses for fighting out of America. The *Sporting Life* is appointed final stakeholder, and the preliminary deposit money of £200 a side staked with the New York *Clipper*, by Mr. Richard K. Fox, on behalf of Kilrain, and the said James Smith, to be forwarded by the editor of that journal to the *Sporting Life* at least two months prior to the day fixed for the fight. The said James Smith and the said Jake Kilrain or his backer (Richard K. Fox), each to have power to appoint an umpire. The referee to be mutually agreed upon by the duly authorized umpires of the men at least seven days before the day fixed for the fight, but in case they cannot agree, the final stakeholder to have power to appoint a referee. The men to be in the ring between the hours of four a. m. and four p. m., or the man absent to forfeit the battle money. The expenses of the ropes and stakes shall be borne by the two contestants equally. The deposits must be staked not later than six o'clock on the days aforesaid, and either party failing to make good the amounts at the time and place named shall forfeit the money down. In case of magisterial interference the referee, if appointed, or the stakeholder, if not, shall (if possible on the same day) name the next time and place of meeting, and either party failing to appear at the time and place specified to lose the battle money. The stakes not to be given up unless by mutual consent, or until fairly won or lost by a fight, and due notice shall be given to both parties of the time and place of giving up the money. In pursuance of this agreement we hereunto subscribe our names.

Witnesses: JAMES SMITH,
J. FLEMING,   RICHARD K. FOX,
JOHN M. BURKE.   (For Jake Kilrain).

After the articles of agreement were drafted both the English champion and his manager read them carefully, and a discussion arose about the time of fighting. Smith desired to fight in three months, while Richard K. Fox proposed that the battle should be decided in January. John Fleming, who was chief spokesman for the redoubtable British champion, after a little confab finally agreed to the proposition, and January 3 was set for the day the rival English and American champions should meet in the ring.

A little debate also took place as to the date of depositing Kilrain's expenses (£100) for fighting out of America. It was eventually agreed that this should be handed over with the final installment of £200 on Friday, Nov. 25, 1887. Then the appointment of referee came on the carpet. Jack Harper at once suggested that it would be advisable to select a referee beforehand. The following discussion then took place:

Mr. Fleming: According to the rules of the prize ring the referee is supposed to be selected independently of any one by the umpires on each side. We select our own umpire and you do the same.

Mr. Atkinson: Yes, that is so; I know that in two or three fights that have been fought over here considerable inconvenience has been experienced in this respect.

Mr. Fox: Would it not be better for the umpires to select a referee at the ring side?

Jem Smith: I have been often disappointed by these "ring side" appointments, If my antagonist doesn't wish to fight, what is more easy for him than to object to all the men proposed for a referee. We could not compel him to decide.

Mr. Atkinson: Shall the referee be appointed by the authorized umpires seven days before the fight, Mr. Fox?

Mr. Fleming: Yes, that is what I wish.

Mr. Fox: I can assure you that the gentleman whom I will choose as our umpire will see that our man does not take any unfair advantage (hear, hear).

After a few remarks Mr. Fox agreed that the referee should be appointed seven days previous to the fight, but should the umpires not be unanimous on their choice, the final stakeholder, the *Sporting Life*, to be empowered with the selection.

The names of several English noblemen and gentlemen of sporting proclivities were then mentioned, and Mr. Fox in his turn mentioned three American gentlemen whom he would be quite satisfied to nominate for the important position of referee. A well-known English baronet, whose name was suggested, elicited from Jem Smith the following remark: "Yes, I'll agree to him. He's a gentleman who understands the job well.' Mr. Atkinson: "I think there are plenty of good men to select from, but there is plenty of time, and it will be as well to leave it to the umpires to decide."

With the concurrence of Mr. Fox, it was next suggested that the attendance should be limited to fifty spectators a side, and this proposition was cordially accepted by the parties concerned.

All these matters having been arranged in the smoothest and most satisfactory manner, Mr. Fleming formally deposited £200, and the bellicose protocol was ratified as heretofore shown, the English champion being the first to append his signature, Mr. Atkinson observing humorously that there was a superstition among pugilists as to signing first.

One of the most important pugilistic conventions of the century having thus been brought to a pleasing and successful termination, a welcome case of Bollinger made its appearance, fittingly accompanied by a box of choice Larrangas. The company being lighted and primed, Mr. Atkinson arose and proposed Mr. Richard K. Fox's health, observing that he hoped the best man would win, and that whatever the issue of the international battle, both contestants and supporters would be as good friends as ever. Mr. Fox cordially reciprocated the sentiment, and remarked that from what he knew of Kilrain, and from what he had seen of Jem Smith, he was quite sure that they would both do their best, and that the winner would be modest in victory, and the loser consoled in defeat.

The festive juice circling freely, some lively chaff and badinage ensued.

"You've a big arm, Jem," observed Mr. Fox, pleasantly.

"It's big enough for some," replied Jem. grimly.

"How old will you be in January?" continued Kilrain's backer.

"I shall be 25 years of age on the 24th of January next; or," continued the English champion with a good-natured smile, "say 24 years on the last 24th of January, it will make me look younger."

"Ah," observed Mr. Fox, "you have the advantage in youth. Jake is five years older."

After the cable announced that the match was made, the announcement created a great sensation throughout England and America. On Aug. 27, 1887, Richard K. Fox, who had been on a tour through Italy, France, Austria and Germany, arrived in London and posted the second deposit. Regarding the event the *Sporting Life*, London, published the following:

Richard K. Fox, proprietor of the New York POLICE GAZETTE, attended at our office yesterday to make good his second deposit of £200 on behalf of Jake Kilrain for his fight against Jem Smith. Shortly before the fourth hour—the appointed time of meeting—Mr. Fox arrived, thus proving good the old adage that "punctuality is the politeness of kings, and newspaper proprietors." One by one the visitors dropped in.

"And how have you been, Mr. Fox?" was inquired.

"Never better in my life; I like your country, and I mean to see all I can of it."

The office clock then struck four, thus proving that Mr. Fox was an honest, veracious and genuine sportsman, and there came trooping in a host of visitors, among whom we may mention the Hon. Peter Westeura, Mr. Wells, proprietor of the Pelican Club; Charles Bates, of the Spread Eagle, Kingsland Road; Col. Keenan, Mr. Fleming, Mr. Pugh, *Cable News*; Bryan G. M'Sweeney, New York; William Baker, Henry Jackson, Sam Blacklock, Mr. Geo. Atkinson, *Sporting Life*, and last but not least, the bold Jack Harper. Several letters of apology were read from influential patrons of the grand old English art. No doubt the division in the House, and the wonderful "spread" at the "Wild West," by Col. Cody, dwarfed the attendance.

"But where is Jem?" inquired the genial Mr. Fox, with his prepossessing smile.

"Oh, Jem will be here in a moment," replied Mr. Fleming, and as he spoke the redoubtable champion entered the room.

Mr. Fox having shaken hands with Jem, remarked, "I think you're getting thinner, Jem."

"No," returned Jem, "I think I am a little bigger."

Then there was a little argument about the "Police Gazette" belt, the gift of Mr. Fox to the winner of the championship of the world. This belt is at present in the hands of Jake Kilrain.

"But," said Jem Smith, "Jake Kilrain has never fought for the championship of the world, and," continued Jem, "it won't be his property until he has beaten me."

A little debate occurred on this subject, and eventually, Mr. Fox said: "Well, Jem, I think you're right; I agree with you that the belt, at the present moment, is the

MITCHELL SMASHES BALDOCK.

A TERRIBLE ROUND.

KILRAIN CONGRATULATED AFTER THE FIGHT.

SMITH BADLY DONE UP AT THE END OF THE STRUGGLE.

neutral or debatable property of you and Jake of course. I allowed Kilrain to hold the belt when he became champion in default of Sullivan putting in an appearance."

" At all events," put in Mr. Fleming, " if Smith and Kilrain are to fight for the possession of this belt would it not be better to leave the trophy in the possession of a third party?"

" Quite so," rejoined Mr. Fox. " When Kilrain lands here he will leave it to the care of Mr. Atkinson, or, if agreeable, we will entrust it to Mr. Wells, the proprietor of the Pelican Club, who will exhibit the coveted prize at the pelicaneries,

"Till the hurly burly's done,
Or the battle's lost or won.'

as Macbeth hath wisely observed before."

All this being satisfactorily arranged the welcome basket of champagne and the box of fragrant smokers made their appearance. The gallant Jack Harper was *facile princeps* with the bottle, and the fragrant cloud being blown freely the strange and singular conjunction seemed to impart a perfect peace to the company.

Mr. Fox broke the beatitudes by observing " Here's my regards, Jem, and I hope Kilrain will beat you."

The noble Jem, who looked as if he'd like to meet Kilrain then and there, said with a contemptuous, defiant air. " If he does I'll make him sore. All I want is to have a comfortable straightforward fight."

Mr. Fox—I admire you, Jem, you and Mr. Fleming have done everything in a straightforward way and I hope that the best man will win.

Smith—I'm sure of it, and that man will be me.

Mr. Fox smiled at the confident air of the champion. At this juncture young Blacklock, the participator of twenty-four boxing competitions (only beaten twice), appeared.

" This pugilist is going to America to take in the nimble ' Yanks ' at nine stone. It is only a fancy of ours but we put it down courageously on paper. They'll have to skip before they take his number down."

" Well," said Mr. Fox, " I want a winner; I've been unfortunate; I backed Paddy Ryan against Sullivan and lost."

" Well," said Smith, " I wish you no harm, Mr. Fox, but I hope you haven't got a winner."

Mr. Fox—If Kilrain loses this fight I'll never back another man. And Mr. Fox frowned as he spoke.

Mr. Atkinson then said to Mr. Fox: " You have heard, I suppose, about the newspaper rumor that Spain objects to the noble art of self-defense? "

Mr. Fox—Do you believe that?

Mr. Fleming, breaking in, " it's all nonsense. I can show you a letter from a gentleman who resides not one hundred miles from Madrid. The affair will take place quietly there; there will be no question of passports; all that, I can assure you, will be arranged. We shall thus avoid the rowdyism that has so long proved a curse to pugilism in this country."

" At all events," said Mr. Fox, " they'll get a bath if they swim there."

After this remark the conversation became general, the general gist of the conversation being as to the composition of the fifty spectators which should accompany each combatant. An eager desire to be amicable was displayed on both sides and it was agreed that each umpire (Mr. Fleming for Smith and William E. Harding, sporting editor of the POLICE GAZETTE, for Kilrain) should have submitted to them the list of spectators on the adversary's side, and should have power of scrutiny. When the exhilarating mixture of champagne had again circled round, Mr. Fox said, pleasantly, " well, Jem, when you have beaten Jake I suppose you'll start a boxing-school."

" No," replied Jem, " I don t much care for boxing, a fighting school is more in my way."

The formal function of staking the second deposit then ensued.

Mr. Fox—" Here is my £200, Mr. Atkinson, on behalf of Kilrain. It's all in bills. I've made it small for you on purpose."

Jem Smith, breaking in—" I don't care how small it is, guv'nor, so as it's all in a lump at the finish." Mr. Fleming then produced a check for £200 on behalf of Jem Smith, and remarked : " No champion of England had ever such a following behind him." At this moment an admirer presented Jem Smith with a very handsome gold-mounted ebony stick, for which the gentle champion returned suitable thanks.

" Kilrain," remarked Mr. Fox, " has the best men in America behind him, and if he wins will receive a present of a thousand dollars from me." " Give me a present, guv'nor, if I win?" said Smith, laughingly, to Mr. Fox. " But I'm not backing you, Jem," remonstrated the proprietor of the POLICE GAZETTE. " Well," said the champion of England as he quaffed his glass, "I make Kilrain a present if he wins. I'll give him this stick which has just been given to me, and I'll put the biggest diamond I can find in the knob." "Here, I'll bet you £50 Smith beats Kilrain," said Mr. Bates. "There'll be plenty of time for betting yet," said Jem, rebukingly to Mr. Bates.

The conversation then turned to Blacklock, who had modestly retired to the background.

"He's a good lad, isn't he?" inquired Mr. Fox of the champion.

"Yes," replied Jem, with his good natured smile; "he'll take his part if they'll give him a chance."

"All I can say is," said Mr. Fleming, chiming in," never had a champion of England such a following as Jem Smith. The Pelicans are behind him. I've not asked for a shilling, and yet I have a thousand pounds in my pocketbook at the present moment to back our champion."

"Well," said Jem Smith, "I haven't the least debut in my own mind, I don't care how cold it is, he'll be warm when he's left off."

To which defiance Mr. Fox replied, "I have grave doubts, Jem; Kilrain will be in the best of condition," and the undaunted Jem retorted shortly—

"Perhaps I'll not be but I'll try."

Again the refreshment urged its wild career and conversational chaos reigned, when eventually a move was made, Mr. Fox said:

"Well, Jem, your friend Mr. Wells, of the Pelican Club, has bet me a case of wine that you win."

"Right," replied the bold and indomitable champion, "and I'll bet you a box of cigars to smoke with the wine." "Well," said Mr. Fox, as he stood in the doorway grasping Jem Smith's hand and smiling pleasantly the while, "you'll do your best and Kilrain will do his best. But win or lose, Jem, count me a friend of yours always."

The ratification of the international prize fight between Jake Kilrain, the American champion, and Jem Smith, the English champion, has created a furore in sporting circles in both hemispheres. Never since the great international battle between John C. Heenan, the "Benicia Boy," and Tom Sayers, the respective champions of England and America, in 1860, has there been a match that has created so much interest or excitement. In bar-rooms, theatres and all pleasure resorts the match is the topic of conversation, and wherever Kilrain, the American champion, travels he is buttonholed and interviewed, while large crowds follow him and look upon him with wonder.

After the special cable from Richard K. Fox arrived stating that the match was made, Kilrain was notified. The champion was stopping at Lakeside, New York. The POLICE GAZETTE correspondent said: "Well, Kilrain, Richard K. Fox has kept his word and matched you to fight Jem Smith, the English champion." "Yes," said the champion, "and I am pleased that the match is made. I knew Mr. Fox would keep his word. I wish it had been John L. Sullivan instead of Jem Smith I had to fight." "Why?" said the POLICE GAZETTE correspondent. "Because I could gain more credit by whipping Sullivan than Smith, and besides it might be an easier task." "Do you think that Smith is superior to Sullivan?" "I cannot say," said the champion, "but the public are well aware that when Richard K. Fox agreed to back Sullivan to fight Smith for $10,000, and agreed that the battle should be fought in Ireland, although Smith agreed to arrange the match, Sullivan backed out. Besides Sheedy, Sullivan's manager, called me a coward and said I was afraid to fight Sullivan and I should have the satisfaction of proving Sheedy a liar, for Sullivan never couldnor never will be able to whip me." "What do you propose to do now that the match is made? What do you think your chances of winning are?" "That is a ticklish question. I think I shall win, if I did not think so I would not allow Mr. Fox to put up $5,000. I am taller than Smith, have a longer reach and will fight at 175 pounds. The advantages, if there are any, are in my favor. If fair play is allowed and the best man wins, I think that trophy (pointing to the "Police Gazette" diamond belt) which represents the championship of the world, will still be in my possession after the battle." "You never fought according to the London prize ring rules?" said the correspondent. "I think," said Kilrain, "they are the best rules to fight by."

On Sept. 8, 1887, Kilrain was tendered a farewell benefit at the Academy of Music, New York, and boxed with Charley Mitchell. On Sept. 19, Kilrain was tendered a similar benefit at Boston and boxed with Charley Mitchell. On Sept. 24, Kilrain and Mitchell call'd at the POLICE GAZETTE office and received, by order of Richard K. Fox, his backer, $1,000, for expenses. The same day Kilrain sailed on the Cunard steamer, with Charley Mitchell and Pony Moore, for England and received a grand send-off and floral tributes.

On Oct. 2, 1887, Kilrain arrived at Liverpool, England, and received a grand reception.

On Oct. 6, the American champion appeared at St. James Hall, London, and was

THE MORNING BATH AFTER THE BATTLE.

THEY HAVE A SMILE TOGETHER ON BOARD OF THE VESSEL.

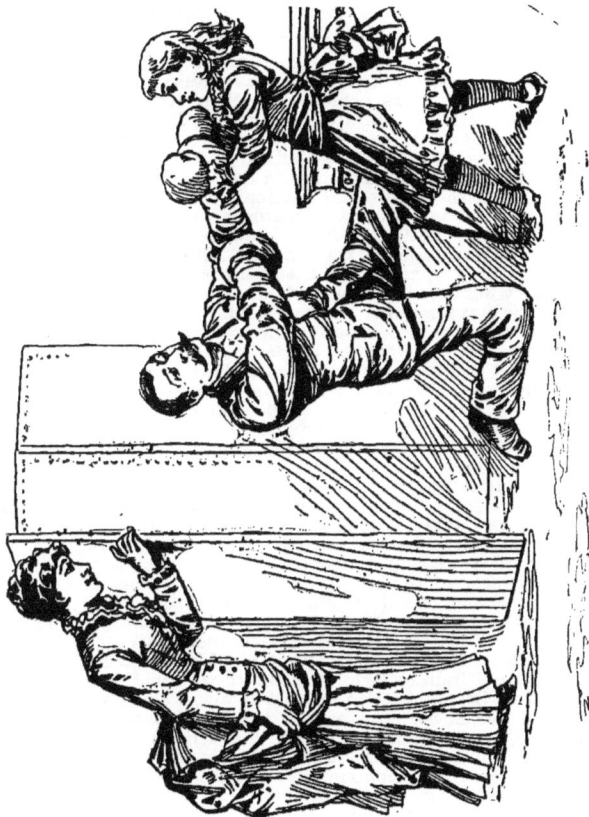

PUTTING ON THE GLOVES WITH PAPA

greeted by an audience of 3,000 persons who gave him a big reception. The "Police Gazette" diamond belt, the first emblem of the heavy-weight pugilistic championship of the world offered in America, was exhibited by Pony Moore and pronounced the most artistic and valuable belt ever put up by any one in England or America.

On Oct. 9, tne Marquis of Queensberry gave a banquet to Jake Kilrain, the American champion, at London, England. On Oct. 10, Richard K. Fox, Kilrain's backer, returned from England. After the match was arranged, a San Francisco paper published the following: If we remember, the Sayers and Heenan fight was the greatest prize battle recorded in the annals of the ring either as regards an exhibition of skill, endurance and downright hard desperate fighting, or in the excitement created by it. In the latter respect it was altogether unparalleled, the interest felt in the match pervading all classes of society on both Hemispheres, and the result being awaited with indescribable eagerness and anxiety by hundreds of thousands of people who ordinarily paid not the slightest attention to the movements of the exponents of the art of self-defence. As soon as the news of the fight reached America the excitement was intense. Places of amusement felt the pressure, and sporting houses and club rooms were thronged by excited people. The fight and the heroic conduct of both principals were the topics of conversation at the family fire side, in the markets, stores—in short, everywhere. Go where we might, fight talk was the rage. Modest damsels, comely matrons and staid and sober pater-familias touched upon the subject, and spoke in condemnation of the action of the referee and the mob by whom he was governed.

Even the Charleston convention was for the time-being forgotten. In fact the excitement eclipsed anything we ever before witnessed in the newspaper world. At Norfolk, Va., a salute of one hundred guns was fired upon the reception of the news, and ministers of the gospel took occasion to allude in sermons next day to the "fair field" whereon the struggle took place. At the time Heenan fought Sayers there was not one half the interest taken in prize-ring matters that there is at the present day, neither did champions have supporters like they have at the present time. Heenan and Sayers, although representative champions of the old and new worlds, only fought for $1,000 a side. Why? Because there was no one in America at that time that had the commixture of Irish pluck to risk $5,000 on the issue of such a contest.

It is a well known fact that the first deposit of $5,000 posted with the New York *Clipper* on behalf of Jake Kilrain to fight Jem Smith was just as large as the stakes John C. Heenan and Tom Sayers battled for. It is also well known that boxers have had backers, but there has never been one in America that would stake as large an amount of money on a champion until Richard K. Fox arrived in this country from Ireland, and with the exception of the championship battle between Yankee Sullivan and Tom Hyer, there never was a champion matched to fight a genuine fistic encounter for the amount of stakes that Kilrain and Smith are to battle for. Review the prize-ring record from Hyer down to Kilrain, and you cannot find that any match—that is, a *bona fide* one—was ever arranged for $5,000 side.

Paddy Ryan and John L. Sullivan fought for $2,500 a side. It would have been for $5,000 a side, for that was the amount Richard K. Fox proposed to match Ryan to mill for, but Sullivan did not have any one to back him for a larger sum than $1,000, and it was only by hook and crook that Sullivan ever found men to put up $2,500, and then Richard K. Fox gave Paddy Ryan $1,000 to bet in the ring, which actually made the contest for $5,000 and an outside bet of $2,000. Looking at the fact that Kilrain and Smith are to battle for $10,000 and the "Police Gazette" diamond belt, and with the surroundings, it would not surprise us if the international battle in which one champion will be girded in the Star Spangled Banner and the other with the Union Jack of England, should create twice the amount of excitement than the Heenan and Sayers battle. No better man than the American gladiator could cross the Atlantic to battle for the Stars and Stripes than Kilrain, and Richard K. Fox made a first class selection.

Many claim that Sullivan should have been selected, but this is foolishness. How could a man that could not be depended upon to meet Charley Mitchell in a boxing match, and who was so intoxicated when it was time for him to enter the ring that he was unable to do so, be matched to battle for $10,000? Sullivan, if we remember correctly, was first selected to be the representative of Richard K. Fox, to go to England to battle as the champion of America against the champion of England, but after the money was posted and the challenge issued was accepted, he refused to meet England's champion. Again, Sullivan has imbibed too freely, he has not paid strict attention to training, and the best man he ever met, Tug Wilson, came within an ace of defeating him. No one has ever conquered Kilrain. In one round he all but defeated Frank Herald, while John L. Sullivan, with the police and referee standing at his back in three 3-minute rounds was unable to conquer Herald and claimed a foul during the contest.

It is true Sullivan has had the title of champion but he kept the title simply because he would not meet his challengers. Dissect his record from the time he whipped crippled Paddy Ryan until he could not conquer Greenfield in Boston, what does ft amount to? Kilrain's battle with Jack Ashton, his great victory over Joe Lannon, who all the ring-followers tipped as a winner, was a better performance than any victory Sullivan ever gained. Why, then, should Sullivan, in place of a genuine champion, which Kilrain is, have been selected to battle for Richard K. Fox's diamond belt and the large stakes of $10,000 and the world's championship?

Richard K. Fox, the backer of Jake Kilrain, made a contract with a well-known silk weaver of Spitalfields to make Jake Kilrain's colors. The following is the banner under which the American will battle for the "Police Gazette" diamond belt, $10,000 and the championship of the world; Kilrain's colors consist of a handsome white silk handkerchief, bordered with red, white and blue. In the left hand upper corner is a shield with the Irish harp and bust of Erin. The right hand upper corner is occupied by the American escutcheon. The left hand lower corner shows the coat-of-arms of Baltimore, the opposite lower corner the armorial bearings of Boston, each in a circle. In the centre is a representation of the terrestrial globe, which is surrounded by a sunburst and reposes on drapery of the Irish and American flags. Instead of the equator the globe is encircled by ropes and stakes, and blazoned on the face of the world is the stalwart figure of Jake Kilrain in ring costume in an attitude of attack. Overhead the American eagle unfolds its wings and carries a scoll in its beak, inscribed "The Champion of the World." The lower quarter of the globe is banded with an ornate legend, which reads: "Jake Kilrain, Holder of the Police Gazette Diamond Belt." All the ornamentation is worked in brilliant colors, making a composition which has never been equalled in the annals of the ring. Mr. Fox selected the design out of several competing drawings, and has issued orders for a reproduction of it regardless of cost or trouble in the very best India silk. The tremendous interest manifested in the coming international battle between Kilrain and Smith is proved, if proof were necessary, by the immense demand already made for copies of the colors. Kilrain's colors are an elegant design, and if he proves the gladiator he is represented to be they will not be trailed in the dust, or will Smith capture them when the battle is over.

JAKE KILRAIN AT HOME.

The *Sunday Sun* of New York says: Every one who has met Jake Kilrain in Great Britian were surprised at his gentlemanly bearing and quiet manner. The English have been so used to tough specimens of the sporting class that to see one who was modest or quiet in his conduct was a revelation. Jake Kilrain, however, has always held a good reputation; in fact, he has been known as "the gentlemanly pugilist." His neat appearance, good clothes, and his tall silk hat, which he always wears, have become familiar to his acquaintances in this country.

In Baltimore, where he lived for nearly two years prior to his fight, he was not only well known but won for himself universal respect. Kilrain's reputation as a trainer while he was still a resident of Boston becoming known to several prominent Baltimoreans, they decided that he was the man they needed to instruct them in the manly art, and, after a short canvass among merchants and club men, it was decided to have a Crib Club, similar to that in Boston, and a committee was sent over to the Hub to secure Kilrain for a trainer. The club soon had a large membership, and Kilrain was installed. The dues for membership were $15 a year, and the instructor furnished each member with twenty lesson tickets for a $10 note. His style of teaching was decidedly different from that of the usual gymnasium instructors; his superb cleverness made him popular, even with his most advanced pupils, and he permitted them to fire away at him to their heart's content. The result was soon apparent in the manner in which the members took care of themselves physically.

He had not been long in Baltimore before he developed a desire for aquatics, and his fancy led him to become the instructor of the Ariel Rowing Club of that city, and for the rest of his stay he creditably filled the two places. As he was well pleased with Baltimore, he brought his family down from Boston and began housekeeping on Wilson street, near Pennsylvania avenue. His family consisted of his wife, a son about two years of age, and a daughter about eight years. He was also accompanied by his sister. The latter is perhaps the most enthusiastic admirer that the great Kilrain ever had, and when he, or "My Johnnie," as his sister called him, was going to fight she could never be convinced that he would not win, whereas Mrs. Kilrain was rather more philosophic, and while she declared Jake to be a great fighter, she always fortified herself in case he was defeated by telling her friends that every man has to meet his master sooner or later. Kilrain takes great delight in his home, and is a kind and proud father.

TRAINING WITH MURPHY.

KILRAIN, JR., THROWS THE BALL.

JAKE AS A DOG FANCIER.

He is a good judge of human nature. He selected for a companion a little red-haired specimen of manhood in Johnny Murphy, of Boston, and had him with him most of the time. Murphy was such a diminutive fellow that the Crib Club members looked incredulous when the big man told them that he was a clever feather-weight fighter, capable of knocking out any of the Baltimore light-weights. To test matters, Billy Young, a fair light-weight was matched to spar Murphy a few rounds with small gloves. The fight took place at the Cribb Club before a select few, and when it was over the little fellow was not bruised, and the Baltimore boy presented a terrible appearance. Two days after the fight the two principals and Kilrain were arrested and, after spending a night at the station house, the three were put under bail. Kilrain's next effort was with a selected scholar of his school, whom he matched with a member of the Baltimore Athletic Club. In this contest his man got done up in short order.

In a prize fight at Point of Rocks between Pete Lally and Al Hartman, two Baltimore middle-weights, Kilrain officiated as timer. In this fight the principals and spectators were naked, as they had to swim a stream to reach the fighting ground. He trained in and near Baltimore for his fights with Jack Ashton, Joe Lannon and Frank Herald, all of which he won. On one occasion Kilrain and Murphy were both training, and went to Druid Hill Park for a run. On reaching the high service reservoir Murphy donned his sweater and started to run, when a son of Erin who was at work near by remarked to Jake that "he ought not to let his son make a fool of himself;" and when Jake started off the man dropped his shovel and yelled out to him: "Sure, and you are a bigger fool than your son." In both clubs he was a great favorite, his peculiarity being his modest demeanor and gentlemanly bearing. Naturally he is one of the best authorities on sporting events, and is exceedingly entertaining, as he can give dates and facts of every prominent event for many years past.

A few weeks before he sailed for Europe he removed his family to New Bedford, Mass., where they now are. In letters to friends in Baltimore he says he will return there to reside permanently, though it is doubtful if he will refuse the tempting offer of instructor for the new athletic club in Boston, which it is said will be tendered him. He is very abstemious in his habits, though inclined to be liberal, and, like John L. Sullivan, he spends money freely. Horses and dogs are hobbies with him. When in Baltimore he owned a handsome English bulldog, which he was always ready to enter for a match; also a large Newfoundland, an inseparable companion of his children. He was a regular attendant at horse races of any kind, and though not generally known, he has driven in trotting matches, and Murphy always claimed for him that he was as clever with the ribbons as with the mittens.

During idle hours at the Cribb Club he endeavored to master the billiard balls, but after months of practice he made but little headway. Tenpins also occupied considerable of his time, but he made little progress at it, and after a few games, most of which he would lose, he would retire to the ring and take his revenge on the punching bag at which he would hammer away in his most vigorous style. While training the Ariel oarsmen Kilrain took advantage of his opportunity to practice swimming, and before last season closed he was expert in the water, and always ready to swim a race with the best swimmer of the club. On one occasion the friendship of the members might have lost him his reputation as a pugilist. He had been in active training for his meeting with Jack Ashton and had received advices that the fight was off, whereupon he accepted an invitation to partake of a soft crab supper with some of the boys.

After a hearty meal he returned to the city and found a telegram ordering him to be ready to fight the next day. The crabs had been eaten, and there was nothing left for him to do but to go on to New York and fight. This he did, and at the expiration of eight rounds had knocked Ashton out. Kilrain has few equals as a feeder.

In his home life Kilrain is an admirable example. Mrs. Kilrain is a woman of medium height and fine physical development, of mild, pleasing appearance, while the baby is a little gladiator, and could throw the round shot long before he could talk. Kilrain's little girl, too, though an exceedingly gentle child, is quite clever with her hands, having gleaned most of her knowledge from instruction given her by Johnny Murphy while with Kilrain.

A GOOD STORY REGARDING THE CHAMPION.

An English correspondent in Staffordshire is authority for the following interesting story of Jake Kilrain and Charley Mitchell, which has gone the rounds:

While Charley Mitchell and Jake Kilrain, the American champion, were bowling through one of the streets in Hanlay, Staffordshire, recently, their trap came in collision with a gypsy wagon, through the carelessness of the sleepy, sunburnt Romany, who was driving, leaving his horses to pick their way through the crowded thoroughfare. The caravan being cumbersome and heavy, laden with pottery and other wares, stood the shock, while the trap's axle was twisted and the wheel dished. The collision aroused the gypsy from his lethargy, and although the accident was his own fault, he roundly abused the occupants of the trap, and Mitchell, seeing the damage done, also vented his spleen on the gypsy. The latter jumped from his canvas-tented wagon, and whip in hand, at once started to horsewhip Charley. He swung the huge black-snake whip with a flourish round his head, preparatory to making a cut at Charley, when the latter quickly grasped the Gyp's arm and, wrenching the whip from his grasp, threw it fifty feet away.

"There is not a man in the counties ever got a whipping like Black Bailey will give yer," the irate man muttered, as he rolled up his jumper to annihilate Mitchell.

Kilrain, who was much amused at the scene, said: "Go on, Charley. One round will do him, and it is the only satisfaction we'll get, for we'll have to settle for repairing the wagon."

"I will give him a good punch anyway and ornament his beautiful mug," Mitchell replied, doubling up his ponderous fists.

By this time two more of the gypsy caravan had come up, and when they looked at the scene one of the drivers, a tall dark-complexioned fellow, held a whispered conversation with Black Bailey. Mitchell, in the meantime, lost no time. He promptly planted a left-hander on the gypsy's victualing department, which only made the latter more furious. He squared himself before Charley, and seemed determined to give as good as he took. Black Bailey was no trifling antagonist. He had whipped many a man in a brawl at the fair and in the village tap-room, but he soon came to the conclusion he had met a tough customer in Mitchell.

The battle was a red hot one while it lasted, but the little Briton made short work of it by knocking the big gypsy down by a tremendous well-directed blow on the ear. He fell like an ox struck with a pole axe.

"You folks will know how to treat gentlemen when you meet them, and not break their trap and then make a bluff to thrash 'em," Mitchell remarked quietly as he took his place beside his companion. "Come, Jake, let us go back and ring changes on the wagon."

"You are not going that way," said the tall gypsy who had witnessed the scene. "you have licked Bailey," but I'm his brother and he's a better knocker than he, though he never would own it. Now, I'll fight you for quits."

Several more of the gypsy cavalcade now came on the scene.

Kilrain said: "My friend has just had all the fighting he wants, but if you want a turn and insist on it, I will accommodate you."

"No, you won't," said the gypsy. "I want satisfaction."

"I will give it to you," spoke up Mitchell, and the next instant a left-hand blow in the stomach, and a terrific right-hander on the jaw sent the Romany to grass. Black Bailey had now come to, and jumping to his feet rushed at Mitchell; but Kilrain stopped the attack and knocked the burly ruffian down. Others now joined the Baileys, and Kilrain and Mitchell had no other alternative but to fight, for there was two to one, and more reinforcements coming. Kilrain had knocked down two of the party, Mitchell had sent another into the hedge-row, when a carriage, in which were friends of Mitchell, arrived on the scene. The Jehu pulled up his leader, for he was driving three horses, when one of the occupants shouted: "Kilrain, you have another match on."

"Yes," said Mitchell, "and it is thick 'un."

The gypsy, on hearing Kilrain's name, at once came to the conclusion that it was the American champion. It is needless to say the turbulent gypsys beat a retreat and left our two heroes to enjoy the joke with their friends.

—